WADSWORTH PHILOSOPHERS SERIES

D1796346

ON

PUTNAM

Keya Maitra
University of North Carolina at Asheville

THOMSON

WADSWORTH

Australia • Canada • Mexico • Singapore • Spain • United Kingdom • United States

Printed in Canada
1 2 3 4 5 6 7 06 05 04 03

Printer: Transcontinental-Louisville

ISBN: 0-534-58400-4

For more information about our
products, contact us at:
**Thomson Learning Academic
Resource Center
1-800-423-0563**

For permission to use material from
this text, contact us by:
**Phone: 1-800-730-2214
Fax: 1-800-731-2215
Web: www.thomsonrights.com**

Asia
Thomson Learning
5 Shenton Way #01-01
UIC Building
Singapore 068808

Australia/New Zealand
Thomson Learning
102 Dodds Street
Southbank, Victoria 3006
Australia

Canada
Nelson
1120 Birchmount Road
Toronto, Ontario M1K 5G4
Canada

Europe/Middle East/South Africa
Thomson Learning
High Holborn House
50-51 Bedford Row
London WC1R 4LR
United Kingdom

Latin America
Thomson Learning
Seneca, 53
Colonia Polanco
11560 Mexico D.F.
Mexico

Spain/Portugal
Paraninfo Thomson Learning
Calle/Magallanes, 25
28015 Madrid, Spain

Table of Contents

Preface

This book is a general and non-technical introduction to some of the major themes in the philosophy of Hilary Putnam. The book is intended for beginning students of philosophy and any one interested in Putnam's ideas. My aim is to provide an accurate representation of Putnam's work which can ground and, more importantly, inspire a more detailed examination of his thought.

Hilary Putnam is one of the major American philosophers of the 20th Century. He has contributed to almost every field of philosophy, giving rise to new movements in some areas, while proposing interesting twists and turns in others. John Passmore, in his *Recent Philosophers* comments that Putnam '*is* the history of recent philosophy in outline' (1988, 97). Putnam has been called the 'Bertrand Russell of contemporary philosophy' not only for his willingness to change his mind on various philosophical topics, but also for his wide range of interests.

Putnam is generally identified as one of the leading 'analytic' philosophers of our time. Practice of philosophy in the analytic tradition is often marked by a need to localize and further a focus on technical matters that often seem remote from larger human concerns. Analytic philosophy is thus contrasted with continental philosophy which is often characterized by more general concerns. Though Putnam begins his philosophical journey deeply entrenched in the analytical tradition, what is truly 'Russellean' about his philosophy is his realization that the dichotomy between analytic and continental philosophies is artificial and simplistic. Putnam's uniqueness lies in his 'infallible instinct for what is genuinely *significant*' and his vision of philosophy that pursues philosophy with a '*human face*'. It is in this that Putnam becomes 'the conscience of our philosophical cultures' (James Conant, in Putnam, 1990, xxxix).

Acknowledgments

Parts of this book draw heavily from a Ph. D. Dissertation that I wrote on Putnam under the advisement of Amitabha DasGupta at the Central University of Hyderabad, India in 1994. I am very grateful to Amitabhada for his valuable guidance and constant encouragement and above all for his faith in my abilities.

I want to acknowledge the support and help that I received from my colleagues in my former Department of Political Science, Economics and Philosophy at the College of Staten Island/CUNY. I am very grateful to my colleagues and friends, Amy Hannon, Carrie Figdor, Dan Kramer, Deborah Popper, Donald Shankweiler, Elise Springer, Mark D. White, Ming Xia, Nancy Fama, Paula Droege, Peter Simpson, Richenda Kramer, Ruth Millikan and Simone Wegge for their help, support and comments at various stages of this project.

My heartfelt thanks to my dear friend and former colleague Chalmers Clark for the countless hours he spent on this manuscript and for his very insightful and helpful comments. Doubtless this book could have been better, but without Chalmers's help surely it would have been worse.

Special thanks to the patient and encouraging Daniel Kolak, the general editor of Wadsworth Philosophers Series. Thanks also to the readers and editors at Wadsworth for their comments.

Special thanks to my parents and family for their love, encouragement and support without which this experience would have been much more difficult and also to my husband, Mohsin, for his love, friendship, support, and his wonderful sense of humor that simply lifts my spirits and keeps me going.

Asheville, North Carolina
July 2002

1
Introduction

... Putnam is, among contemporary analytic philosophers, the one most resembles Russell: not just in intellectual curiosity and willingness to change his mind, but in the breadth of his interests and in the extent of his social and moral concerns.
-- Richard Rorty, *The London Review of Books*

Introducing Putnam

Hilary Putnam is the Cogan University Professor of Philosophy, Emeritus, at Harvard University. He was born in Chicago in 1926. His father, Samuel Putnam, was a well-known author and translator. Putnam graduated from the University of Pennsylvania and then went on to receive his Ph. D. in philosophy in 1951 from UCLA. He is undoubtedly one of the most prominent American philosophers of the 20th century.

If one has heard anything about the philosopher Putnam, it is most likely going to be his 'Russellean' trait as Richard Rorty in the above quotation mentions. He is 'Russellean' in his willingness to 'change his mind' about most issues. In one sense it is true that Putnam has modified and/or abandoned most of the views that he used to hold. Still, in a different sense, I would like to show, his changes are not characteristic of our usual meaning of someone who 'changed their mind'. In order to understand the exact nature of these 'changes' and their implications in Putnam's general philosophical development, we need to look at a few major ideas that have shaped Putnam's thought.

Main Forces and Ideas Shaping Putnam's Philosophy

A unique aspect Putnam's philosophy is how it is developed in response to his visits and revisits of different philosophical paradigms, philosophers, and philosophical debates. It will be useful for our purposes to identify the most prominent of these influences. The first that will be discussed is logical positivism and next is pragmatism. Logical positivism seems most prominent in Putnam's early years since his initial philosophy grows as a critical response to the positivist research agenda. The main theme of Putnam's later works can be characterized as *humanizing* and *renewing* philosophy and what sets the stage here is Putnam's growing appreciation for the American pragmatists.

<u>Logical Positivism</u>

In the early 1900s, a few themes came to prominence in the Western philosophical scene. Foremost among them was the assumption of the centrality of philosophy of language. In this new movement not only are the age-old problems of philosophy seen as merely confusions about language, but all solutions to these problems are conceived in terms of clarifying these linguistic confusions. This shift in philosophy is often called the 'linguistic turn'.

One of the early products of this linguistic revolution was 'logical positivism' – a movement with the aim of applying the methods of science in philosophy. The famous verificationist principle of meaning was a prime result of this movement. According to this principle, the meaning of a sentence is given in its method of verification. That is to say, the meaning of a sentence is determined by whatever observations or experiences show whether or not that sentence is true. For example, the meaning of the sentence, 'grass is green', is contained in the observations and experiences that help us determine whether this sentence is true.

But what happens to our claims like, 'A brother is a male sibling'? No observations seem necessary to determine the truth of this claim. A mere knowledge of the meanings of the terms in this claim seems enough. Further, this sentence seems to remain true, whatever be our experiences as long as the rules of English language remain the same. Interestingly, our mathematical and logical truths seem to have this feature. Positivists used the distinction between the analytic and the synthetic statements to deal with this phenomenon of mathematical and logical truths. While the truth of an analytic statement is determined by its very meaning, like 'a bachelor is an unmarried man', the truth of a synthetic statement is not so determined but is determined rather by the way the world is, like 'grass is green'. This distinction played a crucial role in the logical positivists' research agenda.

When Putnam arrived at the philosophical scene in early 1950s something quite interesting was going on. Almost in all fields of philosophy the main moves were determined by the central research program of logical positivism which was to apply the verificationist principle to each field of philosophy. This program thus consists of a general rejection of traditional philosophical questions, like the nature of the absolute, as meaningless. The reason being that these claims are incapable of verification. The debate between realism and idealism – the two opposing views on the mind-dependence of the world – was also rejected as meaningless and for the same reason: unverifiability.

The central theme of the positivist agenda was a kind of 'scientism', the view that *all* knowledge is scientific. Applying this agenda to various fields, we got 'emotivism' in ethics – the view that ethical judgments like 'one ought to help one's neighbor', in lacking meaning, merely express our emotions (see chapter 7 for more on this). And in mathematics we got 'logisism'– the view that mathematical truths, in order to preserve their meaningfulness, need to be reduced to logical truths.

But the 1950s were also the time when Quine (1951) – a major American philosopher – was popularizing his polemic against the distinction between the analytic and the synthetic on which much of positivism's research agenda relied. Putnam's early philosophy is shaped by a growing dissatisfaction with positivism as a philosophical paradigm. Thus in every field of his philosophy, namely language, physics, mathematics, and mind we see Putnam attempting not only to critique but also to construct an alternative realist research strategy.

Pragmatism

Pragmatism, a distinctly American philosophical theme came to prominence in the early 1900s. Though in its anti-metaphysical spirit, pragmatism is often taken to be indistinguishable from positivism, it grew as a critique also of scientism. What mostly attracted Putnam to the pragmatist camp was its focus on fallibilism. Fallibilism is the idea that in spite of our craving to find the final answer to a question, fresh evidence may present itself to necessitate a change in our view. However, this is not to say that we can *never* know but rather that knowing does not have to involve absolute certainty. Above all Putnam is impressed by the pragmatist perception of philosophy as a 'human' enterprise performed in a community.

Though these two main strands shape Putnam's philosophical outlook, Putnam's relationship to each one of them has been very far from being one of complete acceptance or complete rejection. Thus while accepting the importance of the study of language, and also the theme of philosophy as being continuous with the sciences, Putnam is critical of positivist operationalism where philosophy gets reduced to a study of the techniques of science. Again, while he agrees with the fallibilism of the pragmatists, he is increasingly uncomfortable with at least some of the proponents of pragmatism (for example, William James) in their talk about our 'making up' the world.

What is interesting in Putnam is his concern with the big picture of philosophy. Unlike many of his contemporaries and defying the popular tendency of his time, Putnam always refrains from perceiving or viewing a local problem of philosophy, say in the philosophy of language or in mind or in physics as pervading the entire globe of philosophical concern. It is this eye for the big picture without losing an appreciation for the subtle and technical arguments that best characterizes Putnam's philosophical methodology.

A Concern with Realism

Given the range of fields within philosophy where Putnam has made considerable contributions, the job of writing a book of the present nature that does justice to all those areas of Putnam's contributions becomes exceedingly challenging. However, given the centrality of Putnam's contribution to the topic of realism, I want to organize this book around that topic. Further, the topic of Putnam's realism is the one that has received the most attention within mainstream philosophical discussion.

Traditionally, realism is taken as a metaphysical thesis that argues that the world exists independent of human mind and language and also that the main job of a language and a theory is to describe the world. Realism went out of vogue with the rise of positivism. Putnam's first attempt was to resurrect realism. However, Putnam's interest, since the early days, is not exactly in the metaphysical doctrine of realism as such but in its ability to explain the success of science. Indeed, one of the sources of Putnam's dissatisfaction with verificationists is their rejection of realism.

Putnam argues that such a move sadly leaves the success of science 'as a miracle'. This is because the verificationist operationalism turns out to be explanatorily empty. If truth relies entirely on what we can verify and not necessarily on some correspondence to things in the world, then the enormous success that science has achieved in explaining and predicting various things about the world would seem to be a 'miracle'. In Putnam's hands, realism is transformed into an 'empirical hypothesis', with which he proposes to explain the success of science and also that of general human behavior.

The entire corpus of Putnam's philosophical writing can be perceived as getting clear on this empirical hypothesis of realism and readjustments and shifts that its various implications give rise to. In the realm of the philosophy of language, Putnam's main concern consists of offering a constructive theory of linguistic meaning that can serve as the foundation for the realist hypothesis. In the realm of the philosophy of physics, the main concern consists of fashioning the quantum logic that offers a realist alternative to the verificationism of major quantum physicists in solving the 'interpretation' problem. In the realm of the philosophy of mind, Putnam's approach consists first of an explanation of the nature of a mental state through functionalism and then a move towards direct and natural realism necessitated by his increasing awareness of the centrality of perception to a realist story.

Development of Putnam's Theme: Conversion or Evolution?

In almost every field of philosophy to which Putnam has contributed he has changed his views. Thus the metaphysical realism (the view that the aim of a realist hypothesis is to 'discover' the correct description of the world; see chapter 3 for more on this) of his early days gives way first to internal realism (the view that realist claims of truth and existence can only be made within a conceptual scheme or language; see chapter 3 for more on this) and then to natural realism (the view that endorses the commonsense realism of the common man in arguing that we engage in direct encounters with the world; see chapter 5 for more on this). He also comes to abandon functionalism – a theory about the nature of a mental state. Similarly he rejects the quantum logic of his early days as indefensible. His early views on the nature of the laws of logic and of mathematical truths meet with similar fate. The perceived view of Putnam's philosophy is of one of a 'moving object' that quickly passes from one spot to the next. Some have also complained "Putnam's philosophy [in particular, his swings between realism and anti-realism] is like trying to capture the wind with a fishing net" (Passmore, 1988, 92). How sound is this complaint? Further, given these complaints, Putnam seems to sound like someone who is passing capriciously from one view to another. Is studying Putnam like studying a thinker who is prone to whimsical and frequent 'conversion'?

I will argue that such a characterization is seriously flawed. Consider in this relation, the phenomenon – the 'element of recoil' – that Putnam (1999, 3) takes to characterize a common philosophical reaction to a position that has been shown to have a few problems. What we have seen in the last 2500 years' history of Western

5

philosophy, Putnam writes, is a flight from a frying pan to a fire to a different frying pan to a different fire. Given the charge of frequent change of mind, it might seem that a similar 'element of recoil' characterizes some of the moves Putnam has made especially early on in his philosophical journey. Thus it can be charged that Putnam 'recoiled' from positivism to the robust realism of his 'metaphysical realism' period, then 'recoiling' back from there, for example, to the 'soft' realism of internal realism.

However, as a careful look at the trajectory of Putnam's philosophical development would make it evident, the 'element of recoil' is not what best characterizes his development. What is striking about the 'element of recoil' is the urgency that one feels to run as far as possible from the position that is shown to have shortcomings. This urgent need of complete flight is better captured by the notion of conversion where one denounces a certain position completely to embrace a new and different position. What seems to characterize the development of Putnam's philosophy instead is the idea of *evolution*. [1] What we see in Putnam involves not recoil but a rethinking and readjustment of his ideas. These adjustments may sometimes involve reintroduction of ideas rejected before. Thus while his initial writings are motivated to develop a non-verificationist realism about philosophies of language, mind and physics, his later development of internal realism is an attempt to bring back an element of verificationism into the fold of realism.

While conversions often mark new beginnings, evolution marks changes within a continuous frame. It is the latter model of gradual evolution rather than the former model that seems to me to express the trajectory of Putnam's philosophical development. However, given the main purpose of this book, namely, to introduce the reader to the main themes of Putnam's philosophy, I will not push my argument in any great detail. It is my hope that a careful and impartial presentation of Putnam's ideas is the most forceful argument for this claim. The rest I leave to the readers.

It will also be useful to note how James Conant, a Putnam scholar, characterizes Putnam's shifts. He writes,

> The shift is reflected in a change in the tone of his work: from the authoritative tone of someone explaining the solution to an outstanding problem (functionalism, the causal theory of reference, and so forth) to the unhurried tone of someone who is concerned above all to convey an appreciation of the *difficulty* of the problems. The change in philosophical voice

is from that of someone who is excited to be able to announce that we are on the verge of a revolution (in our thinking about the nature of mind or language or whatever) to that of someone who has become distrustful of such announcements and impressed with how – ... -- those who are unfamiliar with the history of a problem (even its *recent* history) are condemned to repeat that history (in Putnam, 1994c, xii-xiii).

This 'shift in tone' cannot be easily depicted in terms of a number of conversions since what it represents is not a flip-flop between possible alternatives, but rather a transcendence to a higher level where some crucial assumptions underlying the alternatives are unearthed, rejected, and reconstructed. Along with this rejection, the alternatives themselves come to lose their appeal. Further, this shift in tone also expresses Putnam's realization that the peculiarity of philosophical questions is such that they 'consistently tend to outlive the answers that are foisted upon them'.

A challenge that this 'evolution rather than conversion' interpretation of Putnam has to face is to identify a theme that through all the gradual changes remains constant and evolves in his philosophical concern. It seems to me that such a theme can be identified in terms of Putnam's interest in developing a realist picture that explains the 'success of science'. In his metaphysical realist days Putnam had complained that idealism and anti-realism left the success of science 'as a miracle'. He had hoped that metaphysical realism or what he sometimes calls 'scientific realism' would solve that problem. But what he comes to realize later is that scientific realism too fails to explain the success of science. As he writes, "My own view is that the success of science cannot be anything but a puzzle as long as we view concepts and objects as radically independent; that is, as long as we think of 'the world' as an entity that has a fixed nature, determined once and for all, independently of our framework of concepts..." (1990, xx). Interesting to note here that Putnam's notion of the 'success of science' also evolves. Thus while a metaphysical realist is only interested in explaining the success of the so-called *hard sciences* like physics, Putnam's internal realism and natural realism incorporate all *human* sciences in that fold. Likewise, the nature of explanation also evolves from a purely causal picture to that of an interest-relative human image.

A Brief Outline of Chapters

I have devoted a chapter each to the main areas of Putnam's philosophy. You will notice that I have discussed views that Putnam has come to abandon (as in the case of functionalism and metaphysical realism) and/or modify (as in the case of internal realism) later in his writing. So it may be asked if Putnam himself has abandoned and/or modified those views, then what is the purpose of my including them? I offer a two-fold justification for discussing them. First, in many cases Putnam is taken to be the founder of the new view (as in the case of functionalism) and historically speaking, any book on Putnam needs to include those views that he fathered.

Secondly and more importantly, in order to understand the views that Putnam now holds, it is important to realize *how* he got there. In this regard, if we ignore the intermediate views held by Putnam as unimportant, it seems to me we would commit the same kind of mistake that Putnam warns us against: the mistake represented by the 'element of recoil'. A real philosophical insight can be gained by carefully learning where Putnam takes himself to have 'gone astray' and why. Further, given the main theme of this book, which depicts Putnam's work as an evolving picture, rather than a terrain of swift conversions, it is also important that we discuss views that Putnam once held but no longer defends.

It also seems to me that the inclusion of a chapter on moral and political issues needs some justification. Such an inclusion in a book on Putnam might surprise those who are only familiar with Putnam's work on philosophy of language, mind or even physics and mathematics. However, as Putnam's philosophical ideas evolved, moral and social issues have come to occupy a central position in Putnam's general philosophical concern. Putnam's interest in these topics has not developed overnight; neither is it totally coincidental. It reflects a very crucial aspect of Putnam's overall development. This interest grows right out of Putnam's coming to see the interaction between metaphysical and epistemological issues (often considered the core of philosophy) on the one hand and moral and political issues, on the other. Not only does the former shape the nature of the latter, but what Putnam comes to appreciate is that the borders that are often drawn around these different fields of philosophy are artificial and mere reflection of the analytic philosophers' prejudices that pervade the current 'philosophical culture' (Putnam, 1992, 1; see also Putnam, 1999, 69). Hence Putnam issues a call for a 'revitalization' and 'a renewal' (1992, ix) of philosophy in which moral and social issues are taken as importantly as the metaphysical and epistemological ones.

8

Endnotes

[1] The following statement made by Putnam in the introduction of his *Representation and Reality* (1988), which documents one of these shifts, speaks to this issue: "... what I just described as 'changing my mind' is not a matter of 'conversion' from one view to another; it is rather a matter of being torn between opposing views of the nature of philosophy itself. When I was a 'scientific realist,' I felt deeply troubled by the difficulties with scientific realism; having given up scientific realism, I am still tremendously aware of what is appealing about the scientific realist conception of philosophy. I hope that the present book at least partly reveals this 'being torn'" (1988, xii).

2

On Philosophy of Language: Direct Theory of Reference

> Traditional philosophy of language, like much of traditional philosophy, leaves out other people and the world; a better philosophy and a better science of language must encompass both.
>
> -- Hilary Putnam, "The Meaning of 'Meaning'"

Introduction

Putnam's initial focus in the philosophy of language is shaped by an interest to develop a semantics that provides an alternative to the semantics of the positivists. Recall, one of Putnam's main complaints against positivism is that its verificationism fails to support realism. His 'direct theory of reference' is developed as a non-verificationist semantics that would serve the purposes of a realist. In order to understand Putnam's critique of what he calls the traditional theory and his direct reference theory, it is important to understand certain general ideas about semantics.

Semantics, broadly defined, is the study of meaning. But there are very few notions in philosophy as obscure and 'hard' as meaning. Traditionally the word 'meaning' has been used to indicate either of two things, namely, intension and extension. Intension stands for the concept, or the idea attached to a word, or even the general characteristics attached to a term. For example, intension of the term 'water' would include characteristics like colorless, odorless, thirst quenching liquid etc. Extension, on the other hand, stands for the object or class of objects to which the word/term is applicable, for example, samples of liquid we call water.

These two notions are constitutive of any semantic framework that tries to provide an understanding of the relation between language and reality. In an attempt to explicate this relation, a semantic framework tries to explain in clear terms the criteria or conditions of applicability of a name/term to an object or a class of objects.

Traditionally meaning was almost unanimously identified with intension. However, Putnam was among the first philosophers to subject the traditional theory to a systematic criticism by his direct theory of reference.[1] Putnam instead places primary importance on the extension or reference component of a semantic framework.

The Centrality of Intension: An Exposition of Traditional Theory

The traditional appeal of the study of meaning lies in its ability to provide a solution to the problems of synonymity and analyticity. Native speakers of a language use certain expressions as expressing the same thing. This fact is explained through the concept of meaning by maintaining that two expressions express the same thing, i.e., they are synonymous, if they have the same meaning. For example, 'brother' and 'male sibling' are synonymous since they have the same meaning. The concept of meaning is also taken to explain the concept of analyticity. A statement is called analytic if it is true by virtue of its meaning. Thus, the statement 'a bachelor is an unmarried man' is analytic because if you know the meaning of 'bachelor', the truth of this statement will at once be evident to you. In what Putnam calls the 'traditional theory of meaning', the notion of intention or sense is taken to answer both these questions regarding analyticity and synonymity. Two terms are said to be synonymous, if the ideas/concepts/intensions attached to them are the same. Similarly, an analytic statement is taken to be true by virtue of the concepts or ideas involved.

Though different forms of this traditional theory can be identified in the writings of different philosophers, Frege was the first philosopher to formulate it systematically. In "On Sense and Reference" Frege formulates his theory of meaning about proper names (singular terms) and declarative sentences. Frege does not explicitly deal with the meaning of general terms. But given Putnam's focus on the meaning of "natural kind terms", we will discuss the issues of semantics in relation to these terms. A natural kind term is a general term that stands for a class of things that occur in nature. Further, these terms represent "classes whose normal distinguishing characteristics are 'held together' or even explained by deep-lying mechanisms" (Putnam, 1975b, 139). Some common examples would be 'water', 'cat', 'gold', 'acid' etc. as opposed to terms like 'skyscrapers', 'chair' etc., which stand for human artifacts. Frege's treatment of meaning can easily be extended to these terms.

Keeping in line with the traditionalist's intension-extension distinction, Frege distinguishes between the sense and reference of a name/term as the distinction between the mode of presentation of an object and the object presented; the latter being the referent of the expression, the former its sense.

Frege holds that expressions of natural language express senses, and through these senses only they refer to or stand for their respective referents. That is to say, in Frege's opinion the sense of an expression provides us with the route to the object, which the expression stands for. The route to the reference is contained in some descriptive specification of the object. An object satisfying that description will be the object named. This description of the sense of a name is a part of its meaning, and is known or unknown by any speaker with mastery of the name concerned. Reference, thus, does not form a part of meaning. Reference, so conceived, may be considered a consequence of meaning. This central tenet of Frege's scheme can be condensed to his characteristic slogan 'sense (*sinn*) determines reference (*beduetung*)'.

The centrality of sense in this framework, thus, is derivable from the fact that it is taken to supply the criterion for identity and applicability of a name/term. In order to grasp the meaning of a name it is necessary to know the associated criteria of identity and applicability. For example, we may take the name 'Aristotle' which, according to Frege, is logically equivalent to descriptions like 'pupil of Plato', 'the teacher of Alexander the Great', 'the philosopher who was born in Stagira', etc. And these descriptions will give us the 'criteria of identity' in the sense that the object which falls under this set of descriptions will be called by the name 'Aristotle'. The sense of a name, thus, specifies a set of necessary and sufficient conditions to fall under its extension.

Following this discussion, we can formulate Frege's treatment of the meanings of natural kind terms. In this view, the meaning of a natural kind term say, 'lemon' is given by specifying a set (conjunction) of properties which will give us the necessary and sufficient conditions for a membership in that class (i.e., the class of objects called 'lemon').

Putnam's Reformulation of the Traditional Theory

Putnam's critique of the traditional theory subsumes Frege's semantic theory under two features – mentalism and individualism. The main theme of Putnam's critique is to show how these two features run into trouble.

Suppose I ask, how is any speaker going to learn the meaning of a term in the Fregean framework? You reply, well, by 'grasping' the sense of the term, since knowing the meaning consists of knowing the sense. Now to grasp something is ultimately to be involved in some psychological state. Frege himself insists that one gains access to the sense of an expression only by a special mental apprehension. For him 'grasping' or 'apprehending' a sense is a mental process and this is in some ways analogous to visual perception. Frege writes, "[A]lthough the thought [sense] does not belong to the contents of the thinker's [private] consciousness yet something in his consciousness must be aimed at the thought" (1967, 35). This evidently suggests that the grasping of a sense always essentially involves a directed mental/psychological experience.

But since knowledge of meaning in traditional theory consists solely in grasping the intension and grasping is purely a mental act, i.e., an act that can be completed in a person's mind, such knowledge presupposes the existence of no one other than the person grasping it. Thus in this theory, understanding of an expression becomes a wholly internal affair, involving nothing in addition to the speaker but what is directly accessible to her mind. This points our attention to the 'methodological solipsism' presupposed by traditional theory's understanding of the notion of a psychological state. As Putnam defines,

> This assumption [methodological solipsism] is the assumption that no psychological state, properly so called, presupposes the existence of any individual other than the subject to whom the state is ascribed (1975b, 220).

Thus we can reformulate two basic assumptions of the traditional theory of meaning in the following manner: (i) to know the meaning of a term is to be in a psychological state and (ii) the sense of a term determines its extension or reference (Putnam, 1975b, 219). We can attach to these premises the assumption of 'methodological solipsism'. Taking all these presuppositions together Fregean theory comes to consist of the following two features: Mentalism and Individualism.

Mentalism

The traditional theory turns out to be mentalisitc since it implies that whatever goes on *inside* a speaker's mind while grasping a term, is enough to determine the intension (and in turn the reference) of that term. Traditional theory of meaning considers the state of knowing the

13

meaning of a term (say A) as exactly the same as the state of having a mental concept (i.e., to be in a 'psychological state, say S). Further, to be in the psychological state S is also to know that that psychological state is the intension of A. This means that the psychological state S determines the intension of A. This intension in turn determines the extension (or the set of objects referred to) of the term as meaning determines reference. Thus, the psychological state involved in grasping specifies a set of necessary and sufficient conditions to be fulfilled by an object to fall within the 'extension' of that term.

This can easily be seen as an expression of mentalism or psychologism as the psychological states are taken here to be the determining factors. Now, one may point out that Frege argues against the psychological interpretation of his theory on the ground that senses are objective entities, and, therefore, they are not subjective psychological states. But Putnam shows that the very act of grasping these so-called objective senses involves psychologism. The reason is that grasping is solely a mental act. This makes Putnam conclude that, "Frege's argument against psychologism is only an argument against identifying concepts with mental particulars, not with mental entities in general" (1975b, 222). Thus, according to Putnam, the psychologism/Platonism controversy introduced by Frege is "somewhat like a tempest in a teapot" (1975b, 222).

Individualism

According to the traditional theory, to know the meaning of a term is to 'grasp' its intension. But as 'methodological solipsism' makes clear, this does not presuppose the existence of anybody other than the person grasping it. Thus, meaning can be acquired fully in the individual privacy of one's own mental states.

Putnam's Critique

Against this centrality ascribed to sense in the Fregean framework, Putnam proclaims that 'meanings are not in the head'. Putnam's semantics ascribes centrality to reference and to extra-linguistic fact. Let us start with the problems arising from the mentalistic and individualistic scheme of Frege's semantic theory.[2]

Against Mentalism
The Twin Earth Argument

Against the mentalism of traditional theory Putnam offers his Twin Earth argument to point out that extension can never be determined by psychological states. Because "it is possible for two speakers to be in exactly the *same* psychological state, even though the extension of the term A in the idiolect of the one is different from the extension of the term A in the idiolect of the other" (Putnam, 1975b, 222).

To show that 'meanings are not in the head', Putnam gives his imaginative Twin Earth argument (1975b, 223) with the help of a little science fiction. We are asked to imagine that there is a distant planet exactly like Earth in every respect except in some minor points. Let us call this imaginary planet 'Twin Earth'. People on Twin Earth also speak English like us (people on Earth). This 'Twin Earth' differs from Earth in the following feature: on Twin Earth, in place of water, there is a different liquid which is superficially indistinguishable from water on Earth. This liquid has a long and complicated chemical formula and for the present concern Putnam abbreviates it as XYZ. We also imagine that for every speaker on Earth (e.g., S) there is an exact counterpart or *Doppelganger* (S') ("molecule for molecule 'identical'" (1975b, 227)) on Twin Earth whose mental biography is qualitatively the same as that of the given Earth speaker (S). Specifically, we can even imagine that "the same course of non-relational mental associations, events and images run through the minds of any given Earth subject and his or her alien counterpart" (Salmon, 1982, 67).

Now, if a spaceship of Earthians goes to Twin Earth, they will at first think that 'water' has the same meaning on Earth and on Twin Earth. But after discovering the difference between Earth water (H_2O) and Twin Earth water (XYZ) in terms of their chemical composition, the Earthian will say: "on Twin Earth the word 'water' means XYZ". Similarly if a spaceship from "Twin Earth" visits Earth, they will come up with the observation that, "on Earth the word 'water' means H_2O".

In 1994 with the help of advanced chemical theories, it is possible for Earthians and Twin Earthians to make these two above claims about the term 'water'. But we can very well think of 1750 when these chemical compositions of Earth water and Twin Earth water were unknown to us. But it seems intuitively evident that even then by 'water' on Earth we meant H_2O and on Twin Earth we meant XYZ. Here is why this is so.

This is because, as Putnam will argue, Earth speakers only interact with H_2O while Twin Earth speakers only interact with XYZ. Recall also that these two planets are identical in almost all respects and each Earthian can find his counterpart on Twin Earth. We have also imagined that when the Earthian S and the Twin Earthian S' use the word 'water' they are in the same psychological state because they understand it on the basis of its indistinguishable phenomenal features (in the absence of a developed chemical theory). However, the extensions of these two 'waters' of Earth and Twin Earth are different since they are two different liquids. It follows, then, that extension of the term 'water' is not a function of the psychological state of the speaker by itself. Further, meaning (or sense) does not determine extension. Putnam concludes,

> Cut the pie any way you like, 'meanings' just ain't in the *head*! (1975b, 227)

A Green-Colored Lemon is still a Lemon!

The primacy that the traditional theory attaches to sense in providing the criterion of identity and applicability of a term renders any statement of meaning analytic. The reason is, this framework equates meaning with sense and then reduces sense to an exhaustive set of (necessary and sufficient) conditions. This is also because the set of properties associated with the sense of a term becomes logically synonymous with the term. In Putnam's words,

> In the traditional view, the meaning of, say 'lemon', is given by specifying a conjunction of *properties*. For each of these properties, the statement 'lemons have the property P' is an analytic truth; and if P_1, P_2, ..., P_n are all the properties in the conjunction, then 'anything with all of the properties P_1, ..., P_n is a lemon' is likewise an analytic truth (1975b, 140).

If meaning can be given in terms of an analytic definition, then these statements of meaning should express a truth that is both necessary and knowable a priori.[3] And to say that a statement of meaning, say of 'lemon', is necessarily true is to say that in discourse about counterfactual situations the term 'lemon' must apply to just those things, whatever they may be, that have all the features mentioned in the meaning statement. There can be no possible worlds, in which lemons, properly so-called, lack these features. Conversely, in any possible world anything that has all these features is by definition a lemon.

But we can very well think of a few abnormal members of a class which are produced due to some change in conditions or in some other parts. Putnam gives examples of these cases and argues: 'A three-legged tiger is still a tiger', 'A green-colored lemon is still a lemon' (1975b, 140). The problem with traditional theorists is that they cannot accommodate the existence of abnormal members of a natural kind within the range of their theory.

A related problem with the traditional theory is its failure to accommodate scientific change within its framework. Imagine that, owing to some scientific discovery, the things we have been calling cats turn out to be robots controlled from Mars.[4] The robot cats obviously do not have many of the normal properties of an animal cat. Thus it is conceivable, without involving ourselves in contradictions, that cats may lack the properties that traditional theorists take to be analytically tied to the term 'cat'. But if these statements of meanings expressed analytic truths, to conceive cats as robots would involve contradictions. A traditional theorist is forced to maintain that as a result of these discoveries cats cease to exist.[5] But from the point of view of our everyday linguistic practice as well as our scientific practice this conclusion sounds counter-intuitive. As Putnam remarks,

> Even if cats turn out to be robots remotely controlled from Mars we will still call them 'cats'; even if it turns out that the stripes on tigers are painted on to deceive us, we will still call them 'tigers'; even if normal lemons are blue (we have been buying and raising very atypical lemons, but don't know it), they are still lemons (and so are the yellow ones.) Not only will we still *call* them 'cats', they are cats; not only will we still call them 'tigers', they are tigers; not only will we still call them 'lemons', they are lemons. But the fact that a term has several possible uses does not make it a disjunctive term; the mistake is in trying to represent the complex behavior of a natural kind word in something as simple as an analytic definition. (1975b, 143)

These above considerations indicate that the sentences expressing meaning can never be analytic. They express propositions that are neither necessary truths nor truths knowable a priori. Moreover, as a result of Quine's attack on the distinction between the analytic and the synthetic, the traditional theory of meaning seems to lose a lot of its tenability since most of the thrust of the traditional theory of meaning relies on this distinction.

Against Individualism: The 'Division of Linguistic Labor'

Against the 'individualist component' of traditional theory, Putnam proposes his notion of the 'division of linguistic labor'. By this notion he establishes the fact that reference and meaning are social or 'collective' phenomena. So any semantic scheme, which fails to take note of this fact cannot provide a correct model for semantics. We can explain this concept of the 'division of linguistic labor' with the help of the example of gold. In our community gold is important for many reasons. It is a precious and monetary metal, and it is a metal which many people like to wear. We like our wedding rings to be of real gold and not fake. In our community some people wear gold, some people sell gold, some people are engaged in the job of telling whether or not something is really gold. To say this is not to imply that these categories are strictly exclusive in the sense that the person who wears gold cannot sell gold. We are considering it as if it is the 'job' of some people in a community to wear gold and that of some to sell gold and so on. But it is a fact about our society that everyone who buys or wears gold or discusses the 'gold standard' cannot always tell whether something is really gold or not.

Putnam explains this fact by introducing a distinction between *acquiring the use* of the term 'gold' and *acquiring the method of recognizing* whether something is gold or not (1975b, 227). In order to communicate in a society one has to acquire the use of a term. A speaker can do so by acquiring the basic normal characteristics (i.e., the 'stereotype' which will be explained shortly) of the kind that the term represents. But this does not mean that every speaker has to acquire the methods of recognizing whether something belongs to that kind or not. Methods of recognition are a matter of empirical scientific investigation and a few speakers of a linguistic community (the scientific experts in that field) are able to acquire those methods.

In case of doubt about the true extension of a term, a normal speaker can depend on the experts in that field who have acquired the methods of recognizing whether or not a thing belongs to a class. The experts, in turn, determine the extension by conducting different tests. But these tests do not form a part of meaning. Different experts might use different tests. The difference in tests does not matter so long as they pick up the same set of objects as the extension of a term. An expert can select a particular test depending on her convenience, the advancement of scientific findings, etc. As Putnam clarifies the point,

> [T]he test isn't part of the meaning; but that there be some test or other (or something, e.g. a sample, from which one might be derived), is necessary to the preservation of 'the normal usage' (1975b, 151).

In short, Putnam argues every language community divides the 'labor' of acquiring and knowing the use and the extension of at least some terms into two parts. The way of recognizing the extension possessed by the expert is very much a part of the knowledge possessed by the collective linguistic body, even though it is not possessed by each individual of that community. Thus, for example, advanced scientific theory about a term may fall under the social meaning of that term without being known to all speakers who acquire the term. Putnam proposes his 'hypothesis of the Universality of the Division of Linguistic Labor' in the following terms:

> Every linguistic community exemplifies the 'division of linguistic labor'…: that is, possesses at least some terms whose associated 'criteria' are known only to a subset of the speakers who acquire the terms, and whose use by the other speakers depends upon a structured cooperation between them and the speakers in the relevant subsets (1975b, 228).

Frege's individualistic framework, in missing this 'cooperative' aspect of our language use and in insisting that individual psychological states fix the extension flounders as a satisfactory explanation. Putnam summarizes:

> [T]here are two sorts of tools in the world: there are tools like a hammer or a screw-driver which can be used by one person; and there are tools like a steamship which require the cooperative activity of a number of persons to use. Words have been thought too much on the model of the first sort of tool. (1975b, 229)

Reference as Central: Putnam's Direct Theory of Reference

Putnam's critique of the traditional theory shows that the psychological state of grasping the intension of a term does not determine its reference. But the question is, 'how is reference determined, if not by the associated sense'? Putnam's reply to this question is contained in his direct theory of reference.

According to Putnam's direct theory of reference,[6] an initial 'introductory event' fixes reference of a term where the term is 'dubbed' onto the object or a sample of the stuff for the first time. In the initial 'naming ceremony' we 'baptize' what we take to be good examples or paradigms of some substance such as water and then use 'water' to refer to whatever has the same nature as the paradigms. When we introduce the term it is not necessary that we know the nature of the stuff we are naming. Such knowledge will come with empirical scientific investigations. The term, once introduced, can be handed on from person to person in the referential or causal chain, maintaining its original reference at each link.

For example, we can imagine a situation in which the ancient Greeks might be the first people who coined the original cognate of the term 'cat' after perceiving the animal and 'baptized' the animal as such. Then through the causal process involved in communication the Greeks passed on the word 'cat' to the people of later generation. But notice that a link has always been maintained between the Greeks and the later generations since they form an appropriate network of causal relations. Finally, as a result of such process we have received the word 'cat'. Later generations share this reference by being causally connected with the initial 'dubbing ceremony'. The concept of causal chain plays a crucial role in Putnam's scheme.

Let me try to clarify the idea of causal chain by focusing on what constitutes linguistic competence in this causal framework. In the case of the traditional theory, as we have noted above, linguistic competence is explained solely in terms of the knowledge of intension. But, for Putnam, the concept of linguistic competence is not a mentalistic notion. Nor is it a matter of unalloyed knowledge. In this respect he differs from traditionalists and linguists like Chomsky who accept mentalism about linguistic competence.

According to Putnam, linguistic competence consists in the ability to strike the right sort of relationship to certain situations. The right use of a term has to be related to a situation in which the referent of the term was actually present, i.e., in the initial 'dubbing ceremony'. The associated conceptual content of a term/name does not play any necessary role in this initial 'dubbing ceremony' of term introduction. Even if we accept that the associated conceptual content sometimes helps us in picking up the referent, it never provides the ultimate identifying description. To understand the meaning of a term is to be a part of the causal chain, which is after all a social chain, associated with the use of that term.

This point has two main implications -- firstly, it implies that this framework ascribes centrality to the referent (object or class of objects) involved in the initial dubbing ceremony; secondly, it implies that language understanding has a social or collective nature. Putnam's famous concept of the ' division of linguistic labor', as we have noted in our previous section, is an expression of the social aspect of his direct theory of reference.

20

How does one acquire the meaning of a word in Putnam's framework of direct theory? While discussing Putnam's notion of the 'division of linguistic labor' we mentioned that an ordinary speaker of a language learns the meaning of a term by acquiring the 'use', i.e., by acquiring the associated *stereotype*. A stereotype, in Putnam's sense, consists of a few observable characteristics of a normal member of a kind. Thus for example the stereotype of 'tiger' in our linguistic community would include properties like striped, fierce, feline and may be something about size. Any English speaker conveys the meaning of 'tiger' by conveying the above-mentioned features. As you will notice some of these features coincide with the properties included in the meaning statements of the traditional theory. But the crucial difference is that including a feature, say x, in a stereotype of a term 'y' is not to say that 'all ys have x' is an analytic statement. Three-legged tigers are still tigers and as Putnam puts it,

> Discovering that our stereotype has been based on nonnormal or unrepresentative members of a natural kind is not discovering a logical contradiction. If tigers lost their stripes they would not thereby cease to be tigers, nor would butterflies necessarily cease to be butterflies if they lost their wings. (1975b, 250)

An important question to consider while discussing direct theory is how reference makes the criteria of applicability and identity of a term available in this framework. Such criteria are explicated in terms of two factors: first is the object or a sample involved in the initial dubbing ceremony serving as a 'paradigm', and second is the contribution that final sciences, like physics, chemistry and biology etc., make in determining the underlying nature of the referent of the term.

Indexicality and Paradigm

Putnam equates natural kind terms with indexicals. By indexicals, we commonly refer to words that change their extensions from context to context. 'Here', 'Now', 'I' are a few examples of such indexical terms. Interestingly, as Putnam notices, nobody has ever tried to apply the view of traditional theory that 'intension determines extension' to these indexical terms. This is for the obvious reason that no such attempt is going to be successful.

We can make this impossibility explicit with the help of the Twin Earth example. In that example, we have assumed that each one of us on Earth has a counterpart (*doppelganger*) on Twin Earth. And that each Earthian has exactly the same mental make-up as her counterpart

21

on Twin Earth. So, when I think on Earth, 'I have a headache', my counterpart on Twin Earth also thinks 'I have a headache'. But the extension of the particular tokens of 'I' is different in both these Earths. In my verbalized thought the extension of 'I' is myself, whereas the extension of the same token of 'I' in my *doppelganger*'s verbalized thought is herself. Thus the same word 'I' has two different extensions in two different idiolects and since we (myself and my *doppelganger*) are in the same mental state in having the headache, we cannot say that the concepts or intensions associated with that word are different. Putnam, through this example, succeeds in showing that the two assumptions of the traditional theory of meaning -- viz., (a) words have intensions and (b) intension determines extension -- fail to be true in the case of indexical terms.

Putnam summarizes his semantic theory about natural kind terms by maintaining that they (natural kind terms) "have an unnoticed indexical component". The indexicality here follows from two aspects of Putnam's scheme. Firstly, the reference here is determined by tracing a causal chain back to the initial dubbing ceremony that serves as the paradigm. Secondly, it is maintained that the paradigm has to be local, i.e., something from *our* environment. This is because the paradigm has to be something which our forefathers confronted and interacted with while introducing the associated term. By environment, Putnam also refers to the nature of the things (i.e., kinds) themselves. In the example of 'water', the nature of water (H_2O) fixes the reference of 'water'. This indexicality is further clarified by the fact that "... the entire society" as "embedded in its environment" (Putnam, 1990, 110) fixes the reference. Thus, for any sample x, we say that x is water only if x bears the relation of *sameness* to the water *around here*.[7]

Putnam's usual formulation of the direct theory appears to stand in need of emendation as, *prima facie*, it seems to exclude all the *theoretical terms* since it relies on the *observability* of the object in the initial naming ceremony. The emendation can be made by showing that the function of ostensive paradigm is only a *derivative* one. What the user has in mind (battery of referential intensions) under some description or other plays an important role. Such description might have an indexical component in order to provide the spatio-temporal framework within which the descriptive elements single out the intended object. But we should make it clear that the descriptions are in no way synonymous with the terms used. *Reference fixation* is different from *synonymity creation*.

The Contribution of the Final Sciences

This aspect of the direct theory comes to the forefront when we try to determine the nature of the sameness relation mentioned in the ostensive definition of a term. Such a definition of 'water' would say, whatever bears a sameness relation to *this* liquid, while pointing to a glass of water, will be water. The question arises: what sort of sameness, that is, sameness of appearance or of deep structure[8] is being referred to here?

A possible reply might be that it is sameness of appearance that counts. It might be argued that if one's psychological concept of 'water' is so loose as to include not only liquid samples of H_2O but also liquid samples of XYZ, then the term 'water', at least for the speaker, does not designate H_2O, but some general category of liquid with the features colorless, odorless, thirst-quenching etc., which would include samples of both H_2O and XYZ. A challenger of the direct theory might ask, why should we suppose otherwise? Of course, in 1994 almost everybody knows that a liquid sample is a sample of water if and only if it is basically composed of H_2O. But in 1790, in the absence of any such advanced chemical theory, why should we suppose that the term water would properly apply only to samples of H_2O and not of XYZ? That is to say, why should we suppose that it is the sameness of deep (underlying) structure that counts?

Putnam would reply that deep structure sameness must count because even in our ostensive definition we do not rely purely on a sameness of appearance. Here is why. Imagine a person pointing to a glass of water and saying "this liquid is called 'water'". In this case, her "ostensive definition" of 'water' is based on an empirical presupposition. This empirical presupposition is that the body of liquid she is pointing to bears a certain sameness relation to most of the stuff that she and other speakers of her linguistic community have called 'water' on different occasions. This presupposition becomes false if unknowingly instead of pointing to a glass of water she points to a glass of hydrochloric acid. In such cases she does not intend her ostensive definition to be accepted. Thus, we might say that ostensive definitions give us a *defeasible* necessary and sufficient condition for a membership in a kind. But the empirical presupposition on which such ostensive definitions rely ultimately points to a sameness of deep structure.

Putnam further holds that the sameness relation is a 'theoretical relation' which is determined by scientific findings. But deciding sameness with the help of scientific discoveries naturally points to a precondition that the sameness of appearance, which serves at the

23

initial level of naming, should *coincide* with the scientific sameness. But in many respects, this is not the case. Consider, for example, the case of 'jade' as it is found to be associated with two different chemical compounds, namely, jadeite and nephrite. Under such findings, what should be the extension of 'jade'? Or should we maintain the counter-intuitive conclusion that the extension of 'jade' is empty like that of 'unicorn'?

Again, how strict and uniform should this sameness be? We may take Putnam's example of iron. Putnam asks:

> Consider an ordinary sample of iron. By the standards of high school chemistry, it is 'chemically pure'. But it consists of different isotopes. ... Any naturally occurring sample of iron will exhibit the same lawful behavior as any other. But if we use a cyclotron or some other fancy gadget from atomic physics to prepare a sample of iron which is mono-isotopic, that sample will – if the tests are sensitive enough – behave slightly differently from a 'natural' sample. Should we then say that a hunk of iron consisting of a single isotope and a hunk of natural iron are two different substances or one? (1990, 68)

Interest-Relativity in Sameness Determination

All these examples direct our attention to the interest-relativity that Putnam accommodates within the semantics of direct theory. It is true that every semantic framework requires that uniqueness in term-introduction be preserved. We do presuppose while using a term that it will always pick up a unique and the same referent. But, as Stephen Boer (1985, 115) points out, this presupposition is not an indefeasible semantic presupposition. We always readjust our usage following scientific findings. This readjustment is largely interest-relative. In the case of 'jade' the different underlying traits of its referents are accommodated within the linguistic community with the help of some qualifications. What regulate the application of such qualifications are our interests, that is, the purposes that are served by the use of the term. Depending on our social interest, i.e., taking the interest of jewelers into account, we use adjectivally qualified 'true jade' for jadeite as opposed to nephrite jade. Acceptance of this interest-relativity, however, does not "amount to the admission that the original term failed to get any grip on reality". The 'openness' that is allowed to a term largely depends on the various purposes for which a natural kind term is introduced.

What makes room for interest-relativity in the framework of direct reference theory is the collective nature of its conception of language understanding. This collective nature is partly regulated by the 'principle of benefit of doubt'. This principle says that we should grant the introducers or scientists who determine the nature of the referent of a term the possibility of "reasonable modification of his description" (Putnam, 1975b, 275).

"The Meaning of 'Meaning'": Putnam's General Conception of Meaning

Putnam does not want to define 'meaning' by showing it as synonymous with the traditional notion of intension or extension or any thing else. He, instead, provides a *description* of meaning, or to use his expression, 'a normal form for the description of meaning'. His proposal is that this normal form can be given in the form of a finite sequence or 'vector' with at least the following components: (1) *the syntactic markers* that apply to the term, e.g., 'adjective'; (2) *the semantic markers* that apply to the term, e.g., 'natural kind'; (3) a *description* of the additional features of the stereotype, if all of them are not contained in (2); (4) a description of the *extension*. Here is how the normal form description for 'water' would look like according to Putnam (1975b, 269),

Syntactic Markers	Semantic Markers	Stereotype	Extension
Mass noun, Concrete;	*Natural kind; Liquid;*	*Colorless, transparent, tasteless, thirst-quenching; etc.*	*H_2O (Give or take impurities)*

Endnotes

[1] Other major proponents of this theory are Kripke and Donnellan.

[2] Since in his criticism Putnam confines his discussion to natural kind terms, we will confine our discussion to these terms as well. Kripke's *Naming and Necessity* (1980) highlights the problems that

the Fregean framework faces in its treatment of proper names.

[3] This point is also reiterated in Putnam's later writings (e.g., "Why is a Philosopher?" (Putnam, 1990) where he has attributed the problems of traditional conceptualism to its a prioristic nature.

[4] This, like the Twin Earth, is a widely discussed example from Putnam.

[5] Putnam (1975b, 143) mentions that J. Katz maintains this position. Katz has a much nuanced position however implausible. His point is not that cats *cease* to exist but that they *never* existed.

[6] As the name 'direct theory' suggests, the meaning of a term here is taken to be directly associated with the referent, i.e., without any mediation of any necessary description or the Fregean sense. The other name often used for this theory, namely, the 'causal theory' also refers to the fact that a term is taken to refer to that substance that a language user *causally* interacts with in her environment. However, the word 'causal' is not used here in any metaphysically robust sense.

[7] Putnam's view that natural kind terms are indexical and Kripke's view that they are rigid designators can be regarded as two sides of the same coin. Kripke's rigid designator is essentially related to his notion of a possible world. A designator (name or term) is 'rigid' if it refers to the same individual in every possible world in which the designator designates. A kind of necessity thus follows from the possibility of identifying same referent across different possible worlds. Putnam, in his "The Meaning of 'Meaning'" (in 1975b), distinguishes between metaphysical necessity and epistemological necessity and maintains that natural kind terms have metaphysical necessity, whose negation is rationally conceivable. But Putnam clarifies his position further in his later publication, "Is Water Necessarily H_2O?" (in 1990). He identifies metaphysical necessity with 'physical necessity' (1990, 56-7) which has no element of inconceivability. He also distances himself from Kripke especially by giving up all talk about possible worlds (Putnam, 1990, 69). Talk of possible worlds is not a prerequisite for Putnam's semantic scheme due to its empirical nature. As Putnam writes in "Why is a philosopher?" (in 1990), 'no metaphysical glue' fixes the reference.

[8] In his early phase, Putnam takes micro-structure of the paradigm of a kind to determine its nature. But in his later phase he prefers features like 'obeying the same set of laws', 'lawful behavior' (Putnam, 1990, 70) etc., to micro-structure.

3

Humanizing Realism: From Metaphysical Realism to Internal Realism

> ... I think that what is important in philosophy is not just to say, "I reject the realist/antirealist controversy," but to show that (and how) both sides *misrepresent* the lives we live with our concepts.
>
> -- Hilary Putnam, "Realism with a Human Face"

> ... The mind and the world jointly make up the mind and the world.
>
> -- Hilary Putnam, *Reason, Truth and History*

Introduction

The main focus of this chapter is to explain internal realism – the new kind of realism that Putnam introduced in the late 70s as a replacement for his earlier realism which he called the 'metaphysical realism'. Putnam introduces internal realism as an alternative ('a third way') to two philosophical stances that he believes are a Scylla and charybds in philosophy, namely, metaphysical realism and cultural relativism. The stark difference between these two positions comes out clearly when we compare their views on truth. According to traditional realism or 'metaphysical realism', our language and theory 'mirror' the external world and therefore the truth of our claims consists of their resembling (i.e., corresponding to) the things in the world correctly. Cultural relativism, on the other hand, takes truth to be determined solely by the majority's opinion within a culture. Putnam's internal realism borrows aspects from both these views while abandoning what he believes to be their fatal flaws.

While accepting the idea that any realist story must rely on some form of correspondence to the world (i.e., some role of correspondence in the determination of truth), internal realism rejects the impersonal world-view of metaphysical realism. Such impersonality follows since this realist picture of 'mirroring' the world does not leave any room for human rationality to contribute to the realist story. Internal realism, on the other hand, does not 'mirror' reality but constructs it. Internal realism explains our relation to our world by taking into account the role that our language and conceptual schemes play in this relationship. The resulting world-view thus is a *human* one in which we, the speakers, are at the center. This project thus becomes reminiscent of Kant's Copernican Revolution, which said reality should conform to man and not *vice versa*. The point Putnam wants to save from cultural relativism is the apparent truism that we can only speak about the world from within some conceptual scheme or other. However, instead of culturally deconstructing truth in the fashion of a cultural relativist, an internal realist casts truth in ideal terms, more specifically, in terms of an idealization of justification.

I want to show that one way internal realism can be understood is by comparing and contrasting it with metaphysical realism on the one hand and with cultural relativism on the other. I will first present a brief description of metaphysical realism and the main problems that Putnam takes it to face. Next I will provide an outline of internal realism that focuses on the changes that Putnam makes to his earlier metaphysical realism to address these problems. The final part will compare internal realism with cultural relativism.

Roots and Nature of Metaphysical Realism

Putnam's interest in developing a semantic theory was motivated by the need for a theory of meaning that could serve as the basis of a realist metaphysics. We have considered his semantic theory in the last chapter. If we reveal a few realist intuitions underlying this theory, what we get is a kind of metaphysical realism.[1]

In "Language and Reality" (in 1975b), Putnam enumerates two principles – the principle of benefit of doubt and the principle of reasonable ignorance – as two methodological principles of any viable philosophy of language. These two principles govern Putnam's entire theory of meaning and they are realistic in nature. A brief exposition will help in deriving the realist model underlying the semantics of natural kind terms.

The first principle, the principle of benefit of doubt (hereafter PBD) draws our attention to the fact that 'causal theory of reference' uses descriptions *contingently*, i.e., *only* to pick up the referent of a term and does not, therefore, consider it (description) as synonymous with the term. This phenomenon keeps it open for a name to be attached to a wrong description. An initial dubber might want to talk about or refer to a certain object. But due to 'ignorance or inadvertence' the description he uses might not hold true of that referred object. This is mostly the case with scientific terms. With our advancement in scientific findings we might come to realize that the existing description attached to a term does not hold for its referent *in toto*. The PBD says that in such cases we should grant the dubber the possibility of 'reasonable modification of his description'.

For example, according to PBD we should assign the same reference to the term 'electron' which occurs in Bohr's 1900 and 1934 theories in spite of the difference in the informative status of these two theories. Putnam maintains that this principle should be observed as it makes 'stable reference to theoretical entities' possible.[2]

The second principle, the principle of reasonable ignorance (hereafter PRI) focuses on the 'indexicality' or 'the contribution of environment' aspect of Putnam's theory of meaning. Contribution of the environment says that the 'paradigm' of a kind should be a paradigm 'for us' that is, from 'our' environment. Further, the 'actual nature (deep structure) of the paradigm' has to be taken as the final arbiter and even experts might get this wrong. Thus while PBD asserts that meaning is not in the common speaker's head, PRI asserts that it is not in the head of the experts either. The realist intuitions that are implied by these two regulative principles can be enumerated as follows:

1. Both PBD and PRI point to a deeper aspect of Putnam's semantic theory. This aspect consists of his acceptance of theory-independent entities or reality of which our theories give alternative descriptions. This is due to the acceptance of 'the contribution of environment' that says that the 'actual nature of these entities' (paradigm) shape our final meaning of the terms referring to them.

2. The realism underlying natural kind terms accepts an extra-theoretic concept of truth where truth is not an internal affair of a theory but rather an external affair that consists of a unique correspondence to the mind-independent reality.

From these two points the main features of what Putnam calls 'metaphysical realism' can be implied:

3. Related to this above theory of truth (as correspondence) and dependent on it are the ideas of the 'independence' of the world and the 'uniqueness' of *one* True description. (Putnam, 1988, 107).[3] How a conception of truth as correspondence to the reality gives rise to the idea of the 'independence of the world' is not difficult to understand. However, the idea of 'uniqueness' needs more explanation. Uniqueness follows from the fact that since reality has a unique structure and a correspondence to this structure determines truth, there can be exactly one True description of this reality.[4]

4. This metaphysical realist notion of truth also becomes non-epistemic since even the ideal theory may turn out to be false. This is because the intrinsic nature of the external reality (e.g. the existing objects) might turn out to differ from the way it is conceived by our ideal theory. In such case, the world will render our ideal theory false. Truth, thus, may 'outrun the limits of our rationality'.

5. What underlies the unique description of the reality is a determinate and unique reference relation connecting the terms of this description to their referents.

Putnam's Critique of Metaphysical Realism

Putnam tells us two related stories – one short and another long – in criticizing metaphysical realism. Both try to show why metaphysical realism becomes indefensible. In the long story the indefensibility follows when Putnam shows that one of the principal characters become incomprehensible. More specifically, metaphysical realism, in this story, becomes incoherent and indefensible since the unique and determinate reference relation on which the viability of the metaphysical realist picture rests turns out to be 'empty'. In the short story, the indefensibility follows when metaphysical realism becomes 'self-refuting' as it seems to infer its own denial. The longer story is contained in Putnam's 'model-theoretic' arguments while the shorter version is contained in his famous 'Brain in a Vat' argument. Let us start with the short story.

The Short Story: The 'Brain in a Vat' Argument

Here is a brief outline of Putnam's 'Brain in a Vat' scenario. Putnam imagines a world in which the brains of all sentient beings are removed from their heads (by a mad and evil scientist (1981, 5-6; also in 1990, 110) and put in a vat which is controlled by some highly sophisticated computer. The most interesting point about these BIVs (short for the inhabitants of such a 'Brain in a Vat' world) is that they all experience the same mental representations that, we, the non-BIVs experience while interacting with our environment. Putnam attributes this aspect to the impulses from the computer that cause the BIVs to have the illusion that they are having the same experiences as the non-BIVs. Against this background Putnam asks the question, can the words of BIVs (supposing that they also use English which of course is Vat-English) have references in the same way that the words of English (as spoken by non-BIVs) have? That is to say, can a BIV, i.e., an inhabitant of the 'Brain in a vat world', claim, 'I am a Brain in a vat'?

Putnam's reply to this question is an emphatic 'no'. This is due to his direct theory of reference, which argues that the 'causal requirement' must be met for successful reference. To put it in Putnam's words, "one cannot refer to certain kinds of things, e.g. trees, if one has no causal interactions at all with them, or with things in terms of which they can be described" (1981, 16-17). Since the BIVs do not causally interact with brains and vats in their environment, they can't claim that they *are* brains in a vat.

Now, how does the 'Brain in a Vat' scenario become an argument against metaphysical realism? In order to answer this question we need to remind ourselves of two features of metaphysical realism. First, for a metaphysical realist, as we noted above, truth is non-epistemic in the sense that the exact nature of the external world may elude even our best attempts at figuring out this nature. From this nonepistemic perspective the supposition that we may all be brains in a vat seems to present a real possibility. Second, however, a metaphysical realist is likely to accept Putnam's direct theory of reference, which argues that in order to make real claims about certain things in the world we have to be causally related to these things. Now, putting this two points together, a consistent metaphysical realist will have to be able to claim 'I am a brain in a vat' by which she will have to mean a *real* brain in a *real* vat. It is this claim, Putnam argues, that she cannot make. In fact, this failure makes metaphysical realism 'self-refuting' since it forces a *reductio* of the metaphysical realist's premises. I need to explain what a *reductio* is and how it applies to the present case. But let me first give you the argument before explaining how the *reductio* works.

Premise 1: Metaphysical realism is true and truth is radically non-epistemic; we may all be brains in a vat.

Premise 2: For the purpose of referring to an object, we need to be causally (directly or indirectly) connected to it. In other words, "If we were brains in a Vat, we could not consider whether we were brains in a vat" because we are not in the right causal relation to justify such a claim.

Conclusion: So, we are not brains in a vat.

A *reductio ad absurdum* (*reductio* in short) typically shows the absurdity of an argument by showing how an absurd conclusion (often a contradiction of one of its premises) follows from its premises. The *reductio*, in this case, Putnam argues, follows from the fact that neither a BIV nor a non-BIV can make a true claim that 'we are all brains in a vat'. Thus follows the above conclusion, namely, 'we are not brains in a vat' which presents a contradiction of Premise 1 which maintains that we may all be brains in a vat. But why can't a BIV and a non-BIV make the true claim that 'we are brains in a vat'?

Let us consider first why any such BIV claim turns out to be false. Given Putnam's causal requirement as expressed in Premise 2, to refer to trees, brains and vats etc., we need to be causally connected with these things. The BIVs are *ex hypothesie* incapable of any such causal connection since their referential functions are necessarily confined to the range of computer impulses. Thus the BIVs cannot say that they are BIVs in a way in which the non-BIVs can say this (even though the BIVs may have similar mental representations). However, there is a way, as Putnam concedes, in which the sentence, 'I am a brain in a vat' when uttered by a BIV may have a meaning. This sentence as uttered by a BIV essentially means 'I am a brain in a vat in image' or something very similar, but not that 'I am a real (physical) brain in a real (physical) vat'. Thus, this sentence or its collective variant, when uttered by a BIV, results in a false statement. Now, why can't non-BIVs like you and me make this claim truly? This should not be hard to see. When a non-BIV utters the claim, 'I am a brain in a vat', it is definitely false as a non-BIV cannot possibly be a brain in a vat. Thus comes Putnam's final conclusion,

> So, if we are brains in a vat, then the sentence 'We are brains in a vat' says something false (if it says anything). In short, if we are brains in a vat, then [due to reference failure, the claim that]

'We are brains in a vat' is false. [If we are not brains in a vat then 'we are brains in a vat' is of course false.] So it ['we are brains in a vat'] is (necessarily) false (Putnam, 1981, 15).

With the help of this argument Putnam succeeds in showing that on the very assumptions of metaphysical realism, metaphysical realism turns out to be self-refuting. Let me now give you Putnam's longer story against metaphysical realism.

The Long Story: The Model-Theoretic Arguments Against Unique Reference

Putnam's problem with the idea of a unique and determinate reference relation began with his uneasiness regarding the epistemological implications of the concept of a unique correspondence involved in the metaphysical realist world-view. This uneasiness, which Putnam believes dates back to the time of Berkeley and Kant, consists of the worries regarding the possibility of a determinate relationship between two factors – our words, sentences etc., on the one hand and the external world on the other – which do not have any feature in common. For example, ink marks on a page referring to Taj Mahal (i.e., the name 'Taj Mahal') and the building in Agra, India have almost nothing in common. In the same vein, Putnam wonders, How the mind can compare its ideas (representations) with the objects outside. In the absence of any common property shared by both, there can be nothing in which such correspondence may consist. As Putnam says,

> You can't single out a correspondence between two things by just squeezing one of them hard (or doing anything to just one of them); ... (Putnam, 1981, 73).

With the help of the model-theoretic arguments, Putnam argues that unique reference is not possible, nor is unique correspondence. This, in effect, shows the bankruptcy of metaphysical realism.

The Model-theoretic arguments, initially developed in mathematical logic, argue that properties and relations of a formal system can only be studied via their models or different interpretations. Further, model theory reveals that there can be a number of these models each with its own interpretation of the system. Extending this theme to philosophy of language, Putnam argues that languages too can have different models depending on the various different reference relations that may hold.

Why should this pose a problem to the metaphysical realist? The short answer is that a metaphysical realist requires us to be able to single out one unique reference relation from all the possible ones that specifies the real nature of the world. But this, Putnam argues, cannot be done. Let me first explain why it cannot be done before explaining why a metaphysical realist needs such a unique and determinate reference relation.

Ordinarily when we choose from a set of possible hypotheses, models etc., we hold them against certain general principles like coherence, simplicity, generality, truth, predictive power, etc. These principles, which Putnam terms 'operational and theoretical constraints', are what might be called the canons of rationality. However, Putnam argues that these constraints fail to single out one single reference relation since more than one model can satisfy these constraints. As Putnam writes,

> ... no matter what operational and theoretical constraints our practice may impose on our use of a language, there are always *infinitely many different reference relations* (different 'satisfaction relations', ... or different *correspondences*) which satisfy all of the constraints (Putnam, 1983, ix).

Now why should this be a problem for a metaphysical realist?[5] The problem follows from a notion of truth as correspondence that turns out to be non-epistemic. This is because metaphysical realism maintains that even an ideal theory that is fully justified by our canons of rationality might yet turn out to be false. An ideal theory is one which is rationally justified in its ideal limit. The possibility of such an ideal theory's being false can only be explained by the fact that the reference relation used in such a theory is not the 'intended' one, i.e., not the one that corresponds to the real structure of the world. Thus the non-epistemic notion of truth depends on the possibility of there being *the* 'intended' reference relation, which in turn ensures the unique and determinate correspondence relation. The main thrust of Putnam's model-theoretic arguments is that any such intended relation turns out to be empty.

The 'Intended' Relation

Let us assume for the sake of argument that such an 'intended' relation exists. Still, the question is, how is it specified? What is the nature of such a relation? The operational and theoretical constraints obviously fail to capture this 'intended' relation. This is because the operational and theoretical constraints specify our ideal theory. If, in addition, they are taken to specify the 'intended' reference relation then the ideal theory will always have the 'intended' relation. So the very possibility of an ideal theory's going wrong, i.e., having unintended reference, forces a metaphysical realist to accept that there exists some extra feature over and above the operational and theoretical constraints that single out the 'intended' referential relation. Let us for a moment consider a few possible candidates of the intended reference relation as proposed by different metaphysical realists.

One of the candidates offered as determining the unique, intended referential relation is a physical relation/property. A token of a term will refer to any x if x possesses a certain physical property (Putnam, 1989, 216). This proposal, however, does not have much to offer against the model-theoretic arguments since it fails to explain how that particular physical property/relation gets 'singled out'. The upshot of Putnam's model-theoretic arguments is that there exist other physical relations which may as well serve the metaphysical realist's purpose.

A second candidate is the notion of explanation. A proponent of this view would argue that a term refers to a particular object, because it bears a physical relation with it and this relation in turn "... explains the way we behave with those tokens, our observable actions and their observable results ..." (Putnam, 1989, 216-7). Putnam confesses that he thought this was the way out of the model-theoretic problem before he decided to 'go public' with his 'internalist' alternative. However, the mechanism of such an explanatory scheme depends on the fact that certain sentences come out true. So truth is taken to be determining the reference relation. But this involves a 'flagrant circularity' since reference needs to be determined first if we are to consider the possibility of our ideal theory turning out to be false.

Further, the purport of model-theoretic arguments is to show that a theory can be given different interpretations (by assigning different referential relations) all of which preserve the truth-values of the total set of sentences. So any of such reference relations will be able to perform the explanatory role by rendering the entire set true. Thus, the feature of explanation also fails to single out any particular 'intended' reference relation and thereby fails to be the additional constraint that will serve to pick out the 'intended' referential relation.

A 'variant' of explanation as the candidate for determining a unique intended reference is 'causal connection'. A token of a term is said to refer (determinately) to an object when it is 'causally connected' with the latter. Putnam argues against this candidate by using the argument from 'more theory'. The question before us is to determine what identifies the 'intended' reference relation. If we say that 'causal connection' does it, then Putnam wants to ask, what is the referent of 'causal connection' and how is it determined? When the referential relation of the total language is indeterminate, just to offer 'more language' (for example, 'causal connection') as a candidate is simply to beg the question. Further, this candidate also relies on the imprecise, metaphysically problematic notion of causality. Let us, however, be clear about what exactly Putnam is criticizing here.

Putnam draws a distinction between two senses in which a 'theory of reference' can be understood. In one sense, it stands for the way a theory fixes references for its terms (which obviously is an empirical endeavor). In a different sense, 'theory of reference' stands for a theory that deals with the nature and determinateness of the concept of reference, which are a priori questions. Model-theoretic arguments demand an answer for this latter kind of questions. By maintaining that causal connection or causality will fix reference, the realist fails to confront Putnam's real threat. Putnam himself accepts direct or causal theory of reference along with the 'division of linguistic labor' as the right semantic theory of reference fixing. What a realist is required to offer is a reply to the a priori question regarding the nature of reference and not the empirical question of reference determination.

The main trouble with metaphysical realists is that they assume that "what is outside of our mind somehow interprets our language for us" (Putnam, 1989, 219). The task for them is to single out such an interpretation, since, as the model-theoretic arguments show, there can be many such interpretations. Now, since singling out can happen only within a model, there are only two avenues open to a metaphysical realist: either she accepts that minds have 'magical power' that attach our words to their unique referents or she concedes that the intended reference relation is empty. Since no metaphysical realist in the twentieth century believes in magical powers of the mind, the only option available for them seems to be to concede that the 'intended' reference relation turns out to be empty. Since the very intelligibility of the metaphysical realist picture depends on the possibility of this 'intended' reference relation, in the absence of such a relation, metaphysical realist project becomes unintelligible and incoherent (Putnam, 1978, 124).

The real force of Putnam's charge of incoherence becomes evident when we formulate the model-theoretic argument in the form of a *reductio* of the realist premises, more specifically, of the metaphysical realist premise that truth is 'non-epistemic'(Putnam, 1994c, 303) in the same way as in the 'Brain in a Vat' argument. It renders the referential relation presupposed by the metaphysical realist premises indeterminate and empty. It thus poses a *reductio*, since the possibility of a 'determinate referential relation' is a prerequisite of the metaphysical realist picture.

Internal Realism: An Outline

Realizing the internal incoherence of metaphysical realism, Putnam adds the aspect of internality to his earlier realism. Internality points to the fact that our world-views are always conceived in relation to us – language users. The internal realist model is a model from our point of view and not 'from the point of view of the universe'. The given world is *our* world and the realist model too should be envisaged as an attempt to explain *our* interaction with this world. Realism, in Putnam's phrase, thus appears with 'a human face'. The impersonal world-view of metaphysical realism gives way to a more personal interactive world-view. In *Representation and Reality* (1988, 109), Putnam identifies two principal features of internal realism, namely, conceptual relativity and objectivity.

Conceptual Relativity

Conceptual relativity is the direct outcome of the incorporation of internality within the realist model. It is an outcome of Putnam's application of the Lowenheim-Skolem theorem to the field of philosophy of language. It maintains that only in relation to a model or interpretation does our world picture make sense. We can talk about the truth of a sentence or the reference of a term only within the scope of a system of which it is a part. In traditional philosophy, conceptual relativity is usually coupled with some version of conventionalism, the idea that truth and meaning are matters of conventions. While this might be a reason why the prevalent interpretations of internal realism take it as a variant of cultural relativism, we must notice that internal realism does not talk about mere conventionality. It is the world that makes our claims true or false. Reality, for Putnam, is conceived in terms of a 'conventional-factual-continuum' and to do otherwise is to fall into a 'fallacy of division'.[6] As Putnam writes,

> The doctrine of conceptual relativity, in brief, is that while there is an aspect of conventionality and an aspect of fact in everything we say that is true, we fall into hopeless philosophical error if we commit a 'fallacy of division' and conclude that there must be a part of the truth that is the

'conventional part' and a part that is the 'factual part' (Putnam, 1990, x).

Objectivity

The notion of objectivity is reflected in internal realism's concepts of truth and reference. Putnam clarifies that 'objectivity' here does not refer to the traditional objectivity with a capital O. For him traditional objectivity ultimately stands for a perspective-independent 'view from nowhere'. The concepts of truth and reference, within an internal realist framework, do not refer to Correspondence and the unique, determinate relation between our words and the world outside. This, however, does not mean that internal realism rules out our concepts of truth and reference altogether. Internal realism only subsumes them under the scope of a conceptual scheme. Internal realism, contrary to metaphysical realism, does not try to define the concept of reference in terms of an 'essential' and unique relation to the objects outside. Such a priori questions are rejected as senseless. Concepts of reference, meaning, etc., are taken as primitive concepts with many different uses (primitive in the sense of irreducibility). The conceptual relativity of a realist hypothesis consists of the fact that it specifies a particular use for the concepts used in that theory.[7] Internal realism accepts the causal theory of reference as a theory of reference fixing. However, internal realism makes it clear that talking about reference does not specify what reference is in an absolute sense, nor does it maintain that reference is a determinate and unique relation. Reference, on the contrary, is internal to a conceptual scheme.

Truth

Internal realism rejects the 'non-epistemic' concept of truth which relies on the Correspondence relation. The only apparent alternative left for an internal realist might seem to be a coherence theory of truth which takes the truth of a claim to depend on its coherence (compatibility) with other claims of that system and not necessarily in its relation to how the world is.

But it seems to me that internal realism, to be a realism proper, has to include at least some kind of correspondence. Faith in some correspondence is a prerequisite for a realist picture. This is because our pre-philosophical convictions about the meaning of the word 'true' seem to require that a sentence, say, 'grass is green', is true only if grass in the real world is really green. This same pre-philosophical conviction is also reflected in what Crispin Wright calls the 'realist attitude of modesty' that takes truth to incorporate some idea of correspondence of our language to the world. As he puts the point, "... [while making knowledge claims about a mountain], we want it to be a real mountain, not some sort of reification of aspects of ourselves" (Wright, 1988, 25).

Notice however that 'modesty' only reflects the fact that our beliefs are not made true solely on the basis of our ideas. It thus does not warrant a Cartesian-style all or nothing scepticism. Nor does the pre-philosophical understanding of the word 'true' speak in favor of any unique correspondence. Putnam, however, does not dismiss our pre-philosophical convictions about truth (Anderson, 1992,77). Indeed, Putnam's point is that his view of internalized correspondence can explain our pre-philosophic convictions just as well.

The problem that our notion of truth would face, a Correspondence theorist of truth would argue, is that if we give up the 'non-epistemic' correspondence view of truth, truth will then cease to be a regulative principle or normative ideal and become a pure matter of internal justifiability. If we can justify a sentence within our theory then it becomes true. Putnam, however, while agreeing that justifiability (verifiability) and rational acceptability must play a role in our conception of truth, nonetheless retains truth as a regulative ideal. This is reflected in his characterization of truth as an '*idealization* of rational acceptability or justification' (Putnam, 1981, 55, 56). Such idealization keeps the possibility open that even if a sentence is justified in the light of our present day scientific findings, future scientific discoveries might prove it to be wrong and therefore false. That is to say, this sentence might turn out to be wrong in the ideal limit of relevant scientific knowledge. A sentence, thus, to be true, would have to be justified under 'epistemically ideal conditions'. Putnam explains and justifies his insertion of this aspect of 'idealization' in the following terms:

> We speak as if there were such things as epistemically ideal conditions, and we call a statement 'true' if it would be justified under such conditions. 'Epistemically ideal conditions', of course, are like 'frictionless planes': we cannot really attain epistemically ideal conditions, or even be absolutely certain that we have come sufficiently close to them. But frictionless planes cannot really be attained either, and yet talk of frictionless planes has 'cash value' because we can approximate them to a very high degree of approximation (1981, 55).

This insertion of idealization has two major implications: firstly, it distances internal realism from anti-realism and cultural relativism where truth is explicated purely in terms of justifiability. Truth as 'idealization of justification' means that truth is independent of any temporal (individual or collective) justification. Opposed to the cultural relativist notion of truth, it also implies that truth is independent of the belief of the majority of the members of a culture. As Putnam writes,

> Truth cannot simply *be* rational acceptability for one fundamental reason; truth is supposed to be a property of a statement that cannot be lost, whereas justification can be lost. The statement 'The earth is flat' was, very likely, rationally acceptable 3,000 years ago; but it is not rationally acceptable today. Yet it would be wrong to say that 'the earth is flat' was *true* 3,000 years ago; for that would mean that the earth has changed its shape (1981, 55).

Secondly, the 'idealization' also points to the availability of the attitude of 'modesty' in the internal realist framework. The sceptic's worry, as to 'how do we know that we are not BIVs?', when construed within the scope of internal realism, does not express an absolute worry. Even the sceptic's worry is formulated as an internal question. The sceptic's claim is made intelligible as an internal question and then rejected as false.

Thus, this feature of idealization points to the presence of objectivity (with a small o) and correspondence (with a small c) in Putnam's notion of truth. In so doing it stops the reduction of this view of truth to mere conventionalism. Let me explain with the help of an example. Unless we decide upon how we are going to use concepts like 'object', 'existence' etc., the question 'how many objects exist' does not really make any sense. But once we decide the use of these concepts, the answer to the above-mentioned question within that use or 'version', to put it in Nelson Goodman's phrase, is no more a matter of 'convention' (Putnam, 1988, 110, 113). It then becomes a factual question and a reply to it depends on how the facts are and not solely on what we think about them.

Conceptual relativity suggests the dependence of the internal realist notion of truth on its notion of reference. Truth, though explained in terms of idealized justification and rational acceptability, is not reduced to them. Truth and idealized justification, on the other hand, are shown to be 'interdependent' concepts. As Putnam goes on to clarify "... truth is not the bottom line, truth itself gets its life from our criteria of rational acceptability" (Putnam, 1981, 130). These criteria are ultimately tied with the ways in which the words of a language are given referential import. This is what explains the relevance of truth. As Putnam's example shows (Putnam, 1981, 137-8), a person's description of a room will be acceptable as true only if he uses *our* 'concepts' of tables and chairs. Otherwise, his description will not make any sense to us in spite of being formally true. This notion of 'making sense' is made intelligible by the internal realist notion of reference. Putnam writes,

> We can and should insist that some facts are there to be discovered and not legislated by us. But this is something to be said when one has adopted a way of speaking, a language, a 'conceptual scheme.' To talk of 'facts' without specifying the language to be used is to talk of nothing; the word 'fact' no more has its use fixed by the world itself than does the word 'exist' or the word 'object.' (1988, 114)

Internal Realism and Cultural Relativism: A Source of Controversy

Putnam concedes that internal realism has a 'peculiar' nature in being 'the third way' between traditional realism (conceived in terms of metaphysical realism) and relativism. Internal realism is realism with a qualification, namely, the 'internalization' or 'conceptualization' of the realist world-view. This 'peculiar' nature might be responsible for the popular interpretation of internal realism as a kind of relativism.

Relativism in general stands for a view that rejects objectivity (and also absolutism) of any sort. It scorns the idea of objectivity as it maintains, against the realists, that there can be no objective knowledge of realities independent of the knower. Relativists thus accept the conceptual relativity of their world-views. It is this acceptance of the phenomenon of conceptual relativity that brings internal realism and relativism closer and gives rise to the criticism that internal realism is a form of relativism. However, Putnam argues that this interpretation fails to notice that while internal realism can still offer a notion of objectivity and therefore can talk about the possibility of knowledge (taken in the traditional sense), relativism fails to surpass the limitations of conceptual relativity. Since Putnam focuses his critique of relativism on a kind of cultural relativism[8] made popular by Richard Rorty (1980), we will confine our discussion to that version of relativism.

Putnam's main argument against cultural relativism is that it leads to self-refutation. This self-refutation comes about in two different ways. First is an argument which is at least as old as Plato. Basically it says, if everything is relative, the credibility of relativism is also relative. In his criticism of Protagoras, who maintained that man is the measure of all things, Plato showed that relativism can be defeated with the help of its own premise. If, as maintained in relativism, everything is relative, relativism itself becomes relative to our choice, and cannot compel us to accept its views. The self-refutation of relativism, at this level, thus consists in its denial of its own force. Putnam writes,

> Perhaps the shortest [rejection of relativism], though not the least profound, has been wittily phrased by the Californian philosopher Alan Garfinkel. Speaking to his relativist students in their own jargon, he says, 'I know where you're coming from, but, you know, Relativism isn't *true-for-me*'. (1983, 288)

Second, the self-refutation of cultural relativism follows from the incoherence and inconsistency of its own arguments. Putnam formulates his argument from inconsistency against cultural relativism at two levels: one at the level of the cultural relativist's relation to others and the other at the level of the cultural relativist's relation to himself. This argument, when drawn at these two levels, shows that a consistent relativist fails to make sense of what he as well as others say.

Let us begin with how cultural relativists render others as mere 'noise makers'. Cultural relativists ask us to have two stances at the same time. When I say something is true, it is in accordance with the norms of my culture. A consistent cultural relativist goes on to argue, 'when you say something is true, you say it in accordance with the norms of your culture'. But can he really talk about 'your culture'? Isn't 'your culture' equal to 'your culture as seen from my culture' in his framework? If every utterance of mine is tied up with my culture, then my utterances about other cultures are also tied up with the 'norms of my culture'.[9] Thus Putnam concludes, "other cultures become, so to speak, logical constructions out of the procedures and practices" (Putnam, 1983, 237-8) of one's own culture.

Now a thorough relativism expects the relativist to maintain 'your utterances are true in conformity with the norms of your culture'. But this "transcendental claim of a symmetrical situation cannot be understood if the relativist doctrine is right" (Putnam, 1983, 238). The reason is, from our above mentioned argument it becomes clear that a consistent cultural relativist cannot say, 'the status of a person's (other than himself) statement is relative to that person's culture' because by uttering this what he ultimately means is that any statement uttered by anybody (belonging to any culture) is made true by the norms of his culture. Thus, others cease to be 'thinkers' or 'speakers' for a consistent relativist and reduce into mere 'noise makers'.

Now, can a cultural relativist consistently maintain that he can make sense of what he says? Putnam replies, 'No'. When a relativist says, 'X is true', what he means is that 'X is true in relation to my culture'. But even to maintain this consistently, a cultural relativist should be able to say that the statement 'X is true for person P' or for himself has a strict, definite and absolute meaning. To utter this a relativist has to accept an absolute notion of truth. A consistent relativist cannot do this.

In the absence of such definite or absolute standard, a relativist's language will fail to make any sense since such a relativist will be left with no distinction between 'being right' and 'thinking he is right'. This point, which Putnam thinks has its germ in Plato's criticism of Protagoras, was 'brilliantly extended' by Wittgenstein in his Private Language Argument. This argument maintains that a person, who cannot go beyond his own sensations, will not have any standard to differentiate between 'being right' and 'thinking to be right'. To maintain this distinction meaningfully, the relativist should accept an "intelligible notion of *objective* 'fit'" (Putnam, 1981, 123); or as Wittgenstein maintains, the concept of 'criteria'. As a relativist cannot have this notion of objective fit, he fails to avail himself of this distinction. A consistent relativist will therefore be left with no distinction between 'asserting' or 'thinking' and 'making noise' (or 'producing mental images') (Putnam, 1981, 122; see also Putnam, 1990, 23-29). This reduces a relativist to a mere animal and accepting this reduction is to 'commit mental suicide'.

Further, the incoherence of cultural relativism follows from the '*praxis* of the Relativists themselves'. Most relativists know that their cultural peers aren't convinced by their arguments. But they keep on arguing because they themselves think that justification or warrantedness goes beyond majority option. As Putnam writes, "To tell us that Galileo had 'incommensurable' notions *and then go on to describe them at length* is totally incoherent" (1983, 193).

Putnam agrees that the norms and standards that we use to judge a sentence's idealized warrantedness are not absolute; rather they are 'historical objects' 'evolving in time'. However, while a cultural relativist takes this 'historicity' as a mark of pure communal nature of justification, Putnam wants to retain objectivity (understood internally).

It is this point that sets Putnam's internal realism apart from cultural relativism. As he writes,

> The fact is not just that we *do* change our norms and standards, but that doing so is often an improvement. An improvement judged from where? From within *our* picture of the world, of course. But from within that picture itself, *we* say that 'better' isn't the same as '*we* think it's better.' And if my 'cultural peers' don't agree with me, sometimes I *still* say 'better' (or 'worse'). There are times when, as Stanley Cavell puts it, I 'rest on myself as my foundation' (1990, 26).

So, how does Putnam's internal realism relate to metaphysical realism on the one hand and cultural relativism on the other? Let me conclude with the following quote which seems to capture the main thread of Putnam's reply:

> I take it as a fact of life that there is a sense in which the task of philosophy is to overcome metaphysics and a sense in which its task is to continue metaphysical discussion. ... *Of course* philosophical problems are unsolvable; but as Stanley Cavell once remarked, 'there are better and worse ways of thinking about them' (Putnam, 1990, 19).

Endnotes

[1] It needs to be clarified that for Putnam realism has never been a purely metaphysical doctrine, in the sense of building an a priori picture of the world. Realism is conceived as presenting an empirical hypothesis (though not in the strict scientific sense of hypothesis) to explain the phenomena we observe (Putnam, 1975b, 21; also see his John Locke Lectures, in Putnam 1978). Putnam in his "Why is a Philosopher?" observes that his realism is different from the traditional realism which was held by the traditional theory of meaning. As he says, "[T]his [his new or direct theory of reference] kind of 'realism' goes with a more fallibilistic spirit in philosophy" (Putnam, 1990, 110). Still, as will be discussed shortly in the text, what becomes metaphysical in this empirical realism of Putnam is his faith that our language succeeds in giving One True Correct picture of the mind-independent world.

[2] The application of PBD is however not unreasonable. It is

applicable to 'electron' but not to 'phlogiston'. The reason is, in the case of 'phlogiston' no 'reasonable reformulation' of its original description is available that can turn into a characterization of a kind of entity that we recognize.

[3] Later in his *Dewey Lectures 1994*, Putnam characterizes metaphysical realism as a view that maintains that there is a 'definite Totality of All things with a definite Totality of All properties'. This presents another way of formulating his previous characterization.

[4] Even if there are more than one descriptions of the world, they all must turn out to be versions of one single description.

[5] More specifically, Model-theoretic arguments were the results of Putnam's attempt to extend the implications of Lowenheim-Skolem paradox in mathematics to philosophy of language.

Let me explain this paradox and the theorem that resolves it briefly. Cantor proved that reals are non-denumerable (uncountable). Skolem's theory in mathematics, on the other hand, argues that every consistent non-empty theory has a denumerable (countable) model. Skolem held that even Cantor's theory, as it is a consistent theory, can be interpreted over a countable model. Thus results a paradoxical situation that the reals are both countable and uncountable.

This paradox was resolved by Skolem in his model-theoretic response (in Lowenheim-Skolem theorem) with the help of the concept of a 'referential shift'. This resolution says that a formalized theory can be given different interpretations, i.e., models depending on the referential relation chosen. The apparent paradox is due to the misconception that terms used in our mathematical theory can be given absolute definition irrespective of any model/interpretation we assume. Skolem's point is that the terms of a theory can only be defined internally, within a model, for any particular interpretation. How do this paradox and the model-theoretic response arise in the philosophy of language according to Putnam?

Putnam answers that a somewhat similar kind of paradox arises in any metaphysical realist world-view when we try to single out the 'intended' reference relation from a number of possible ones. The only resolution, Putnam argues, would be to stop looking for such an intended relation. As he writes,

I shall argue that it [the 'Lowenheim-Skolem paradox'] *is* an antinomy, or something close to it, in *philosophy of language*. Moreover, I shall argue that the resolution of the antinomy – the only resolution that I myself can see as making sense – has profound implications for the great metaphysical dispute about realism which has always been the central dispute in the philosophy of language (1983, 1).

[6] We commit the 'fallacy of division' when we argue from the fact that some properties are true of a thing considered as a whole, to the conclusion that the same are true of parts of that whole. Consider for example the property of 'extinguishing fire'. While this property is true of water, it does not hold true of water's parts or elements, namely, hydrogen and oxygen. In fact oxygen aids fire! And hydrogen is the gas that blew up the Hindenburg!

[7] Internal realism, owing to its adherence to conceptual relativity, adds one more normative constraint to its regulative ideal of the 'Principle of the Benefit of Doubt': that the comparable theories should treat ('use') the concept of reference in a similar fashion. This aspect is evident in Putnam's comment that "[M]eanings have an identity through time but no essence" (Putnam, 1986, 11). That is to say, they should be identifiable as using the same concept of reference in order to apply the Principle of the Benefit of Doubt to them.

[8] In his introduction to *Consequences of Pragmatism* Rorty (1982) changes his outlook on truth from his view in *Philosophy and the Mirror of Nature*. In the latter work he defined truth as 'intersubjective acceptability in a culture' (hence the name cultural relativism). In the former work Rorty presents his position on truth by taking it as a purely formal (and therefore empty) notion devoid of any content that can be specified in terms of correspondence to the world. To say "'snow is white' is true" is just to *say* 'snow is white' in a different way. However, while rejecting truth, he still holds that what we are interested in "is whether a sentence or whole discourse pays its way by the standards of our fellow 'postmodern bourgeois liberals'" (Putnam, 1994c, 331). Since this change in detail does not affect the main critical force of Putnam's arguments I have not discussed it in this text.

[9] Putnam draws the full implication of this argument with the aid of the following reasoning:

..., suppose R.R.[Richard Rorty], a cultural relativist, says:

When Karl says 'schnee ist weiss', what Karl means (whether he knows it or not) is that snow is white as determined by the norms of Karl's culture (Putnam, 1983, 237). Karl's culture is a German culture. But in R.R.'s statement, the truth gets defined in relation to his own cultural norms, namely, that of American culture. So we get Putnam's restatement of R.R.'s statement:

> When Karl says 'Schnee ist weiss', what he means (whether he knows it or not) is that it is true as determined by the norms of American culture that it is true as determined by the norms of German culture that snow is white (Putnam. 1983, 237).

4

On Philosophy of Mind: Functionalism and Beyond

> The purpose ... is to argue that mental states are not only compositionally plastic (the same 'mental state' can, in principle, be a property of systems which are not of the same physical constitution) but *computationally* plastic as well—the same mental state (e.g., the same belief or desire) can in principle be a property of systems which are not of the same computational structure.
>
> -- Hilary Putnam, *Representation and Reality*

Introduction

Setting the Stage

As Putnam says, functionalism has become the 'orthodoxy' in the contemporary philosophy of mind (1994c, 441). Given its popularity, it is intriguing to note that Putnam has come to abandon this position of which h e i s c onsidered a s o ne of the main founders. But in order to understand the attraction of functionalism and Putnam's reasons for abandoning this position, it is important to review some of the historical events that brought functionalism about.

The Mind-Body Problem

One of the perennial problems of philosophy is the mind-body problem. Here is a n on-technical way o f u nderstanding t his p roblem: We generally make two sorts of statements about people. The first kind is the physical statements that we make about a person's body, physical states, dispositions etc. For example, 'Johny has six fingers in his right hand'. Statements of this kind can also be made about any physical object whatsoever. For example, 'this table has three legs'. The second kind of statements is the mentalistic ones where we talk about a person's thoughts, desires, hopes, feelings, personality etc. For example, 'Johny hopes to get a fire truck for Christmas'. We further think that these statements can only be made about humans and probably about some higher animals. At the outset these two kinds of statements are very different and there isn't any apparent translation available of one into the other. So the problem is to figure out whether these two kinds of statements are about two different kinds of metaphysical stuff or are they just two ways of talking about the same stuff.

Historically this became a 'problem' once Descartes introduced his dualism that argues that mind and matter (or body) are two completely different substances without sharing anything in common. Once the dualism came into place, the questions regarding the different natures of the substances became pressing. Descartes argued that mind and body are two independent substances in the sense that one can exist without the other. The mental substance is non-extended and thinking whereas the physical substance is extended and unthinking. Further, with the increasing mathematization of nature, in the seventeenth century, the stark difference between the mental realm and the physical realm came to the forefront. Descartes' argument was that given the essential difference in their natures, mental entities couldn't be understood by any method applicable to our understanding of the physical entities.

Of course Descartes had his critics and one of the most pressing problems that Descartes' dualism faced is the problem of mental and physical interaction: if the mind and the body are so very different then how do we explain the appearance of interaction between them which we all experience? When you *want* to drink water (a mental event), you *walk* to the water cooler (a physical event). Attempts to explain this interaction brought a host of related questions under the umbrella of the so-called, 'mind-body problem'. One such question is, (A) 'what is the nature of a mental state?' Another related question is, (B) how do we individuate a mental state or how we identify a thought as a thought or what makes a pain a pain? With the increasing dissatisfaction of psychologists to study these questions only introspectively, i.e., by looking at one's own minds – the only method available to a Cartesian dualist – the dualist scheme itself came under attack.

What motivated and intensified this attack on the mental-physical divide is the arrival of behaviorism in the intellectual scene. Gilbert Ryle (1949), for example, argued that Descartes' mind is nothing but a 'ghost [i.e., non-existent] in a machine'. Behaviorists argued that there is nothing more to the mind than the person's observable behavior and dispositions to behave in a way under certain circumstances. Thus for example, for Anna to be in pain is nothing more than for her to behave in a certain way, namely, wincing, groaning, and looking for pain medication etc. or disposition to behave in that way if there was nothing to stop her from doing so. The main point in the behaviorist thesis is that there is nothing to the Cartesian story of Anna's having inner episodes or an inner life in having pains, sensations, or thoughts. All of the so-called mental realm can be explained by the subject's observable behavior and dispositions to behave in characteristic ways.

It is not difficult to see the problems with behaviorism. First of all, it seems to leave out some real and important items that we all are conscious of which seem to be quite different from, and therefore not captured by, our behavior and our dispositions to behave. Take for example the feelings of calm and serenity that I experience when I look at a beautiful sunset. Is the *feeling* of calm fully explained by my disposition to smile and to say things like, 'how lovely'? Further, we can imagine two people who may differ psychologically while their actual and counterfactual behavior might be exactly the same. A zombie might behave exactly the same way you do without sharing any of your (or anyone else's) mental states.

Identity theory emerges as a 'happy' compromise between the metaphysical excess of Cartesian dualism and the metaphysical deflationism of behaviorism. Deriving lessons from empirical identities like 'lightning is a particular kind of electric discharge', an identity theorist[1] argues that a mental state is *identical* with a state in the central nervous system. Unlike the behaviorists, the identity theorists accept that at least some of our mental realm does involve inner states that are episodic, but instead of giving those states a non-physical status, like the Cartesians, they argue that these inner mental states are nothing but (i.e., identical with) the states occurring in the subject's central nervous system or more specifically, the brain. Thus for Anna to be in pain is to have a certain neuron (philosophers' celebrated example, the c-fibre) firing in her brain.

Putnam's entry into this philosophical landscape is through his criticism of the identity theory. Putnam pointed out an implication that makes this view very restrictive. Say we make 'being in pain' identical with 'having one's c-fibre's firing in one's brain'. Then it will follow that for any creature anywhere to be in pain is to have her c-fibre's firing in her brain. But to think this is not only gratuitous but also indefensible. Why should we think that a being has to share our neuro-chemical structure in order to have something that can be recognized as pain (Putnam, 1960)? Identity theorists, in order to correct the deflationism of behaviorism seem to land themselves in 'species chauvinism', i.e., the view that being in pain or having any other sensation or mental state, requires one to be a member of the biological species of *homo sapiens*.

Formulation of Functionalism

Putnam identifies the problem with the identity theory as implicit in the view that "the essence of our minds is our 'hardware'" (1988, xii) which drove them to think that "our *what* is more important than our *how*" (1988, xii). Putnam provides a new way of thinking about the mental, by pointing out that our function is more important than our matter. Thus we get 'functionalism' that argues that our mental states are identical to functional states. Now, what exactly is a functional state? Is it a state with a function? Yes and No. As it turns out, it really depends on what you mean by 'function'.

Ordinarily speaking, the term 'function' gets associated with ideas like purpose, reason etc. This sense of the term has gained popularity especially since the advent of the literature on biological functions. Thus, we say the function of the heart is to pump blood. It is also true that some philosophers like Eliot Sober, take 'functionalism' to imply this concept of a biological function. However, instead of understanding the function of a state in strict terms of the purpose it serves, Putnam here understands it in terms of how it relates to and interacts with certain other factors. In this regard, its use is like the mathematician's use of the term 'function' where the term stands for mapping or a method of transformation. Thus, when a mathematician says, 'y is a function of x', what she means is that the value of x determines the value of y through various functional forms like $y=2x$, $y=x^2$, $y=x/2$ etc. 'Functional' in this sense stands for 'computational', or as we will see, 'logical'. This should come as no surprise because the basic theme of Putnam's brand of functionalism consists of conceiving the human mind in terms of a computational model. More specifically, using the model of a Turing machine, Putnam argues that a mental state is explained or described by its role in the program of such a machine. The program, in this case, describes the psychology which explains how the mental state relates to and interacts with various environmental factors, and also with other mental states.

The Idea of a Turing Machine

Putnam clarifies that a functional state is a state of a Turing machine. But what is a Turing machine? Alan Turing was a mathematical logician who is credited as the father of computers. He talked about a 'machine'[2] while explaining his theory of computation. Turing machine is an input-output device with a finite number of internal configurations. Turing's original idea of this machine is that of a typewriter with the following features:

(a) a tape which is divided into separate squares on each of which a symbol (drawn from a fixed finite set of alphabets) may be printed.
(b) a 'scanner' that gets the input by 'scanning' one square of the tape at a time.
(c) Finally, a printing mechanism that erases the symbol appearing on a particular square and prints a new one.

Here is how the machine works: it gets an input (i.e., its scanner says a particular symbol appears on one of the squares), it responds by erasing the symbol on the tape and writing a new symbol from the finite set on it and going into a different state or staying in the same state. The way machine performs this is drawn from the description in the form of a *machine table* that specifies how a given state is related to input, output and other states of the machine. A machine table consists of intersecting columns and rows where the columns represent the states and rows represent the inputs and each square has an 'instruction' written on it that tells how to generate the output. Any machine that is describable and/or described by a machine table is a Turing machine. Our ordinary Coke machine can provide us with a good example of how a primitive Turing machine works.[3] Using a diagram taken from Ned Block, we can present the machine table describing a Coke machine as follows:

	S_1	S_2
Nickel Input	Emit no output Go to S_2	Emit a Coke Go to S_1
Dime Input	Emit a Coke Stay in S_1	Emit a Coke and a nickel Go to S_1

According to this machine table, State S_1 and State S_2 can be described as the dime-desire and nickel-desire respectively. Of course no one is suggesting that the Coke machines have real desires but it exemplifies rather nicely how analogous although much more complicated machine tables involving desires, etc. would work.

The Basic Moves of Putnam's Functionalism

Functionalism provides a 'computational theory of mind' in that it argues that human beings are analogous to computers and our psychological states are functional states, "that is, they are the states that would figure in an ideal description of our 'program' [machine table]" (Putnam, 1994, 507). However, after first proposing this view in his 1960 article "Mind and Machine", Putnam later modified the view and finally rejected it entirely in 1988. It will be helpful to take note of these various stages because this will give us a sense of the intuitions that made functionalism plausible and also of those problems that finally convinced Putnam to leave this 'ism' behind.

In short, a Turing machine state is such that when given an input, it gives out an output and goes into another state. And the 'program' (mapped in terms of the machine table) that Turing talked about is such that it explains the relationship of the various states of this machine to various inputs and outputs and also to each other. In identifying a functional state with a Turing machine state, Putnam identifies a psychological state with a Turing machine state. However, he comes to realize that while transition in Turing machine states is deterministic, in the case of a human being it is often probabilistic. Faced with this problem Putnam comes to explicate the idea of a functional state in terms of a state of a 'Probabilistic Automaton'. Putnam further assumes that these Probabilistic automata are equipped with sense organs (and states corresponding to 'sensory inputs') and motor organs (and states corresponding to possible 'behavior outputs'). At this point Putnam presents the main theme of his functionalist hypothesis in terms of the following two theses:

(1) All organisms capable of feeling pain are Probabilistic Automata.[4]

(2) Every organism capable of feeling pain possesses at least one Probabilistic Automaton Description (specifying the functional states of the Automaton and the transition probabilities between them) of a certain kind (i.e., being Capable of feeling pain *is* possessing an appropriate kind of functional organization). (1994, 508-9)

Notice that at this stage Putnam identifies a functional state with a Probabilistic Automaton state and *not* simply with a Turing machine states. However, he soon comes to realize that functional states cannot be identified with machine states of any kind since human psychological states are quite different from either a Turing machine or

53

a Probabilistic Automaton states. That's when he comes to explicate the functional state in terms of a 'description that will be provided by an ideal psychological theory' (Putnam, 1994, 510). Putnam further claims that constructing such a theory forms 'an inevitable part of the program of psychology' (1975b, 435).

Here is Putnam's basic theme of functionalism in a nutshell: He argues that a psychological state can be understood in terms of a complex network of relations, namely, between the sort of sensory input that caused it, the kind of behavioral output it causes and the other mental states it gives rise to. Take for example the case of a pain in my hand. The sensory input that might have given rise to this pain state is a pin prick, the behavioral output is wincing, ouching, etc., and this state typically also gives rise to some other mental state, in this case, a desire to get rid of the pain, wanting to see a doctor, etc. As in the case of a Turing machine state where the associated program (machine table) gives us the complex network of inputs, outputs and relation to other states, in the case of a psychological state the 'program' specified by the psychological theory determines the complex network that specifies the functional role of this state. It will be useful to recapitulate here Putnam's main functionalist moves.

(a) First proposal: psychological states are *identical* with Turing machine states.
(b) Modification I: Psychological states are identical with Probabilistic Automaton states.
(c) Final Modification: psychological states are not identical but are *analogous* to functional states and the 'program' will be given by the ideal psychological theory (which we will work out in 200 years and constitute the main program of psychology).

Functionalism and the Identity Theory: Compared and Contrasted

The Hope of Multiple Realizability

From our above description we are now in a position to see the main difference between functionalism and behaviorism. While the functionalist computational model of the mind does take behaviors into account, in its explication of the nature of psychological states, it doesn't try to *reduce* these states into pure behavioral states. However, the difference between Putnam's functionalism and identity theory may not be so easily discernable. The main difference here lies at the level of abstraction involved in their respective descriptions of a mental state: while an identity theorist identifies a mental state with a physical (brain) state, Putnam identifies (or makes analogous) such a state with a functional state described in terms of a functional description. What is special about a functional description is that it never specifies the nature of the physical system that realizes that description. The question of realizability remains open. In fact, as Putnam writes,

> …, the 'logical description' of a Turing machine does not include any specification of the *physical nature* of these 'states' – or indeed, of the physical nature of the whole system. (Shall it consist of electronic relays, of cardboard, of human clerks sitting at desks, or what?) In other words, a given 'Turing machine' is an *abstract* machine which may be physically realized in an almost infinite number of different ways (1975b, 371).

Thus in insisting that one does not have to share our biology in order to feel pain, functionalism avoids the 'species chauvinism' problem that troubled the identity theorists. Further, functionalism opens up the possibility that different systems, say a human being, a hydraulic computer and a digital computer, all turn out to be 'psychologically isomorphic' in that they all are 'instantiations' of the same psychological theory in different physical mediums. This aspect surely gives functionalism a lot of flexibility and also explains its enormous popularity. But why did Putnam come to abandon this position?

Problems with Functionalism

We have noted Putnam's constant modification of the basic functionalist thesis. The main reason for this is his realization that human functional states have certain properties that are not shared by any machine states. This motivates Putnam, as we have seen, to make the human functional states *analogous* and not identical to machine states.

But this is not the only problem facing the functionalist thesis of Putnam. Functionalism in its present form turns out to be inconsistent with the direct theory of reference proposed by Putnam. In order to understand this criticism, we need to look at how functionalism tries to answer the question mentioned above, namely, 'How do we individuate a mental state'? In arguing that a mental state is identical with (or analogous to) a functional or computational state, Putnam answers this question by claiming that a mental state should be identified or individuated by its role in the 'program' that describes the computational (psychological) theory. In doing so this functional role also determines the intentional content of this state, or, crudely speaking, what the state is about.

Now as we have seen in our chapter on reference, according to the direct theory of reference, the meaning or reference of a term is not determined solely by what lies inside one's mind but at least partly by one's relation to one's environment and other members of one's language community. But this idea seems to be incompatible with the functionalist theme. If a psychological state can be individuated or identified by its functional role then its content seems to be entirely determined by its functional role. But, functional role does not include one's environment but simply the sensory input, behavioral output and relations to other mental states. Using the example of Twin Earth, we can say that the Earth Tom and Twin Earth Tom are in the same mental state in believing that water is cooling, when considered in terms of their functional state. Because, as we have seen, the difference between Earth Tom and Twin Earth Tom does not lie at the level of what goes on inside their heads, which would include, sensory inputs, relations to other mental states and behavioral outputs. The difference lies at the level of the liquid substance that is present in their respective environments. So it seems as though while direct theory argues that Earth Tom and Twin Earth Tom have different beliefs (or beliefs with different contents), functionalism would argue that they both have the same belief (since their beliefs are functionally indistinguishable).

Putnam gets around the problem of direct reference failure by introducing what he calls 'sociofunctionalism' (Putnam borrows the idea first suggested by Richard Boyd). According to sociofunctionalism, our description of the ideal psychological theory is not only a theory of one isolated individual but "a theory of a group of organisms, and has to include a description of their interactions *with one another and with their environment*, and of the nature of the relevant parts of the environments." (Putnam, 1994, 511, emphasis added; see also 1988, 74 -76).

But the real trouble with functionalism came for Putnam when he tried to formulate the psychological theory that is supposed to supply the much-needed functionalist 'program'. As Putnam himself recounts the matter in his self-portrait as a functionalist (1994), he soon came to see how difficult it was to come up with a theory that could serve the role of a Probabilistic Automaton description. The difficulty lies in the fact that while the Turing machine description (or the Probabilistic Automaton description) identifies each machine state by distinguishing it from *all* other states of that machine, it is difficult to imagine that any psychological theory (however ideal) can provide such a complete description for each of the mental states for every one of us. As Putnam writes,

> No one has ever claimed to provide a theory in which so much information about the state of believing, say, that there are cows in Romania, and about the connections between that state and other psychological states, and between all of these states and 'sensory inputs' and 'behavioral outputs', is provided as to *individuate* the state of believing that there are cows in Romania (Putnam, 1994, 510).

Not only can we not identify all the mental states of a person in relation to which the functional role of a given state is to be determined, but too often a given state is related to a number of different beliefs, etc., in different people. This brings us to a further problem with sociofunctionalism.

We have noted above that sociofunctionalism extends the purely computational story of earlier functionalism to include physical as well as environmental properties as determinants of the intentional content of a mental state. This, in short, is a project to reduce the concept of intentionality into physical and/or computational properties. This proposed reduction, however, presupposes the possibility of there being an unique set of physical and/or computational properties which will determine the intentional content of a mental state and thus be analogous to the latter. But as Putnam points out, even when you and I (or any two speakers of English) have the same belief, say, that the cat is on the mat, we may not be in the same computational cum physical state. This is because we may have different stereotypes of cats, have different beliefs about the nature of cats, etc. This is also because, as neurologists have told us, the number of neurons in one human brain is almost always different from that of another brain. Similarly, no two human brains are 'wired' the same way.[5]

Thus, there always is a plurality of physical and/or computational properties that a given mental state can be reduced to. Putnam realizes that just as our mental states are 'compositionally plastic', they also turn out to be '*computationally* plastic'. Further, "mental states cannot literally be 'programs,' because physically possible systems may be in the same mental state while having unlike 'programs'" (Putnam, 1988, xiv). Putnam clarifies the point by acknowledging that,

> ... the very arguments I formerly used to show that a simpleminded identification of mental states with physical-chemical states cannot be right, can be generalized and extended to show that a straight-forward identification of mental states with *functional* states, i.e., with computationally characterized states, also cannot be right. (1988, xii).

Putnam asks,

> When we are correctly described by an infinity of logically possible 'functional descriptions,' what is the claim supposed to *mean* that one of these has the (unrecognizable) property of being our 'normative' description? Is it supposed to describe, in some way, our very *essence*? (1988, xv)

Multiplicity of these various candidate functionalist descriptions defeats the functionalist agenda. It also brings out an interesting and problematic aspect of functionalism. While functionalism was initially introduced as a counter to the physicalist reductionism of the identity theorists (namely, that a mental state *is* a physio-chemical or brain state), it itself turns out to be reductionist in its own way.[6] It is true, as Putnam argues, anything (including even a disembodied spirit) can be taken as having mental states when it can realize the functional organization. Still, in attempting to reduce a mental state to a computational or computational and/or physical state, the functionalist project becomes reductionist.

Moreover, this reductionism, unlike the reductionism in physics, turns out to rely on 'Utopian speculation'. In physics we have managed to confirm that "the laws of reduced optics, to the extent that they were true, were explained by the fact that the 'light rays' and 'light waves' they spoke of were really electromagnetic radiation of certain wavelengths" (Putnam, 1994, 509). Putnam's functionalist reductionism bases itself on the *hope* that future psychological theory will help us confirm that "the laws of unreduced psychology, to the extent they are true, will be explained by the fact that the psychological states they speak of are really these functional states" (1994, 509). Success of this explanation *of course* depends on figuring out 'a normal form for the psychological description of organisms'. But as we have noted above, it is impossible to get a psychological description of a human being, let alone of 'an *arbitrary* organism' that could serve the functionalist purpose. This Utopian reductionism also represents what Putnam calls 'scientism', an attempt to take science at face value, i.e., 'without reinterpretation'.

So, what sort of a thing is a mental state? Putnam answers that human mental states are 'emergent from and may be supervenient upon computational states' (1988, xiii) without being identical and/or analogous to them. Further, intentionality – the ofness or aboutness that our mental states enjoy – turns out to be a non-reducible property of our mental life with many different possible uses or interpretations. Once Putnam became clear about the hidden reductionist agenda of his own former functionalist self, he abandoned that position whose only defense, he realized, could come from psychology's impossible 'craving to be like physics'.

Endnotes

[1] The Australian philosopher J. J. C. Smart (1962) is one of the earliest champions of the identity theory.

[2] I put the word 'machine' in scare quotes here since Turing did not devise a machine in any concrete sense of the term. His contribution lies in the fact that he explained how a computational 'program' would run.

[3] Though Turing in his initial description of his machine and also Putnam in his 1960 essay explains the concepts of 'machine' and machine tables in terms of a tape machine, since the coke machine example seems to capture the idea, while explaining the basic notion in a simpler way, I have decided to use this example.

[4] Though Putnam formulates his thesis in terms of pain he clearly believes at this point that this hypothesis can be applied to all cases of psychological states.

[5] This is because such 'wiring' depends on 'maturational history and environmental stimulations' to a given brain (Putnam, 1988, 82).

[6] It is interesting to note in this regard that though Putnam proposes functionalism as an alternative to physicalist reductionalism, many philosophers in the literature have taken functionalism to prove or show that physicalism is true.

5

Liberating Realism:
From Internal Realism to
Natural Realism

> Winning through to natural realism is seeing the
> *needlessness* and the *unintelligibility* of a picture that
> imposes an interface between ourselves and the world. It is a
> way of completing the task of philosophy, the task that John
> Wisdom once called a 'journey from the familiar to the
> familiar'.
>
> -- Hilary Putnam, *The Threefold Cord: Mind, Body, and World*

Yet Another *Kind* of Realism? Why?

Is Putnam offering another *kind* of realism in the form of natural
realism?[1] The answer I would suggest is Yes and No. To see this
consider the question that comes under Putnam's critical attention at
this stage: 'how does our language hook onto the world'? Putnam's
simple answer to this question is that it is an ill-conceived question and
that realism needs to be rescued from it. Thus natural realism is *not*
another kind of realism in the sense of offering another alternative way
of answering the question about language's hooking on to the world.
However, it *is* a kind of realism in the sense, as Putnam will go on to
argue, that it is the only viable form of realism that should interest a
philosopher. Let me explain. First, we will need to review a couple of
main moves that Putnam has made so far.

In his metaphysical realism period what Putnam is interested in is
an empirical hypothesis of realism which aims at explaining the success
of science and in general the relation between language and reality.

60

What we get here is a realist hypothesis which relies on the causal-explanatory notions of truth and reference. In spite of its empirical nature what turns out to be *metaphysical* about this picture, as Putnam comes to note in his internal realism phase, is that in taking science at 'face value' (i.e., without reinterpretation), metaphysical realism looks to science as the ultimate arbiter of philosophical problems. But since there are many true stories, how can science help us identify *the* unique and 'intended' true story? Soon this interest in realism which Putnam later characterizes as realism with the capital R, is replaced by an interest in realism with the small r, namely, internal realism.

An internal realist argues that we can't get out of our skin, so to speak. In other words, we cannot get out of our language or conceptual scheme. Thus, while a metaphysical realist argues that our cognitive powers (i.e., our abilities to think about, imagine and conceive the world), get hooked onto the world mysteriously, an internal realist argues that such powers cannot reach all the way to the objects themselves. It is this underlying assumption of both metaphysical and internal realism about the nature and limits of our cognitive powers that Putnam comes to question in his natural realism. What is realistic about Putnam's natural realism is not its interest in constructing a 'realist hypothesis' but its 'realist spirit'.

The most striking feature of Putnam's natural realism is his growing appreciation of two features. First, an appreciation of the fact that what drives both metaphysical realism and even a Rortian kind of cultural relativism is a concern about 'losing the world' (1994a, 446). Second, an appreciation of the fact that the internal realist's attempt to transcend this worry fails because a very basic presupposition of it goes unchallenged. This presupposition has to do with the way our conception about the nature of our mind shapes the realism-relativism debate. What becomes Putnam's main focus in formulating natural realism is to articulate this presupposition and clearly explain the troubles that it invites. Let us consider these two features carefully.

Can we really 'Lose the World'?

A metaphysical realist in her haste to capture the world as it is *in itself* ends up endowing the world with a 'magical power' by which the world bestows the intended reference and correspondence relations to our language. The motivating concern quite naturally is that otherwise we will fail to get a hold of the world and in the end 'lose it'. What is interesting to note in this regard, Putnam tells us, is that a very similar worry motivates a cultural realist like Richard Rorty. Now this may seem counter-intuitive. A relativist, we think, cannot be worried to lose the world since she is not interested in getting to *the* world in the first place. Putnam wants to show otherwise.

As we noted in our chapter on internal realism, cultural relativism turns out to be inconsistent and incoherent. This is because, as Putnam's arguments show, a cultural relativist cannot treat others as well as himself as 'speakers'. The cultural relativist ends up treating 'speakers' as 'mere noise makers'. Putnam identifies the ultimate cause of this predicament in the relativist's inherent 'craving for objectivity'. Lurking right under this craving is a kind of scepticism which worries that we might not be able to capture the world in its true color. The contribution that a relativist makes to this worry is to assert that none of our descriptions captures the world in its true light. From this a relativist concludes that all our descriptions and interpretations are relative and that there is no longer any room left for truth.

Here is another way of making this point. The success of metaphysical realism, as we noted, depends on our ability to compare our words and language with reality as it is in itself. Cultural relativism argues that any such comparison turns out to be 'unintelligible' and therefore impossible. But in deriving the impossibility of our words to be about the world from the *unintelligibility* of this comparison, Putnam argues, a cultural relativist has in fact assumed the intelligibility of this comparison! As Putnam puts the point,

> ... if we agree that it is *unintelligible* to say, 'We sometimes succeed in comparing our language and thought with reality as it is in itself,' then we should realize that it is also unintelligible to say, 'it is *impossible* to stand outside and compare our thought and language with the world'. Rorty seems to be telling us of an impotence, in the way the physicist tells us of an impotence when he says, 'You can't build a personal motion machine,' but it turns out on examination that the impotence is a mirage, or even less than a mirage—that it is chimerical (1994c, 299).

Putnam notices a 'trace of a disappointed metaphysical realist impulse' in Rorty's haste to reject any possibility of our language to be about the world. Thus in constructing their theories in response to their worry about losing the world and in depending on the idea that the other is the 'only alternative' (Putnam, 1999, 13), both the metaphysical realist and the Rortian relativist 'mirror' each other. As Putnam notes,

Failing to inquire into the character of the unintelligibility which vitiates metaphysical realism, Rorty remains blind to the way in which his own rejection of metaphysical realism partakes of the same unintelligibility. The way in which skepticism is the flip side of a craving for an unintelligible kind of certainty has rarely been more sharply illustrated than by Rorty's complacent willingness to give up on the (platitudinous) idea that language can represent something which is itself outside of language. While I agree with Rorty that metaphysical realism is unintelligible, to stop with that point without going on to recover our ordinary notion of representation (and of a world of things to be represented) is to fail to complete the journey 'from the familiar to the familiar' that is the true task of philosophy (1994c, 300).

According to Putnam, this nihilism about truth and fear of scepticism can surely be avoided if one is not driven by the 'craving for objectivity' or by the worry to 'lose the world'. But how to transcend this craving and this worry?

Internal realism tries to transcend this craving by arguing that reference relations and correspondence relations can only be made from within the perspective of a language and conceptual scheme. What internal realism tries to do is to combine an aspect of cultural relativism (namely, conceptual relativity) with an aspect of metaphysical realism (namely, objectivity). However, what internal realism fails to notice is that it still operates within the confines of traditional epistemology.

This epistemology, given to us by the seventeenth century modern philosophers, takes a division and therefore an interface between observers and the world as the basic starting point. You might wonder, 'But, didn't we leave this problematic epistemology behind by moving away from the Cartesian dualism?' That is to say, by our rejection of the division that Descartes posited between our minds and our bodies? Putnam would reply that the legacy of this interface in epistemology is still with us. But to see how this is so, Putnam argues, we need to look carefully at the kind of philosophy of mind that is presupposed by the frameworks of metaphysical realism and relativism.

Realism and the Nature of Mind

You will recall that Putnam's move to internal realism was provoked by his recognition of the epistemological problems that were implied by the metaphysical realist picture. His turn to natural realism is similarly provoked by his realization of the epistemological implications that a given philosophy of mind has when combined with realism. Putnam writes, "...the question of realism [namely, 'how does our mind or language hook on to the world?'] cannot be discussed without entering explicitly or implicitly into an account of mind" (1994c, 295). What one needs is not just to have a theory of mind, but to look carefully at how that theory shapes the way one poses the 'question of realism' and the alternatives one considers possible.

This becomes evident from the fact that Putnam all along had a theory of mind through his metaphysical realism and the internal realism period. As we noted in our last chapter, it is *functionalism* and it considers the mind to be a functional organization. But what Putnam hadn't considered up until his natural realism period is the epistemological implications of functionalism especially for our conception of realism. Putnam comes to see that

> ...our difficulty in seeing how our minds can be in genuine contact with the 'external' world is, in large part, the product of a disastrous idea that has haunted Western philosophy since the seventeenth century, the idea that perception [and knowledge] involves *an interface between the mind and the 'external' objects we perceive* [and make knowledge claims about] (1999, 43, emphasis added).

This realization leads ultimately to the rejection of this epistemology along with its grounding philosophy of mind. But how does this epistemology come into place?

Let us start with a brief overview of the Cartesian epistemology. This epistemology relies on the dualistic picture of the mental realm and the physical realm (which contains objects like bodies). The mental realm is the realm of consciousness which is inhabited by various mental states whose ingredients have been variously called 'ideas', 'impressions', 'sensations' etc. Further, this view argues that mind can only be conscious of and therefore know what lies within the realm of consciousness. This leads to the received view of perception that we can only perceive directly that which is within the mind. If this is true, then the question that becomes pressing is, what happens to my claim of, say, seeing the chair in front of me? Further what happens to my claim of knowing that there is a chair in front of me? Chairs, tables, rabbits and in short, the world, is not in my mind. So I can't know them directly.

It follows that there has to be an *interface* – an intermediate meeting point – between my mind or more specifically my cognitive powers and the 'external' world if any perception and knowledge of the external world is to be possible (Putnam, 1999, 10, 12). But still this interface can produce only an *indirect* knowledge of the world. In seventeenth century Western philosophy, Putnam tells us, this picture of an interface not only explained how our perception works but also how our conception works. I will return to it in a moment. Notice here though that this epistemology of an interface between mind and the world has determined the nature and extent of realism as well as idealism. Thus we have Berkeley arguing that since we can know only our ideas, only our ideas exist. Locke and Descartes, on the other hand, argue that we do know, though indirectly, that the external world exists as the cause of our ideas, sensations, and thoughts etc.

What has happened with the so-called celebrated rejection of 'the Cartesian picture'? What about the materialist's ultimate triumph over dualism? Putnam replies that the arguments bringing about this rejection do not really touch the interface epistemology. The rejection of the Cartesian picture has only been effective at rejecting the idea that inner mental states are immaterial and nonphysical. So the popular idea now is that inner mental states are physical states of our brains. Still, our cognitive powers, our powers to know, and see and think, are still confined to what lies within us. Thus what remains of the Cartesian picture is the idea that the mind still is within us and can only know the world *indirectly*.

Consider the popular view about how we think about things. Conceiving or thinking is very much like building and/or manipulating mental pictures or mental representations of the things in the world. What makes these representations about the world is their causal relations to the things in the world. Putnam's example of imagining a deer in the meadow shows quite nicely how we still retain the Cartesian interface theme:

> Imagining the deer—let us assume that 'visual imagery' is involved—is traditionally conceived of as the formation of something in every way analogous to a picture, except that the picture happens to be 'mental.' This 'mental picture' is supposed to play exactly the role that 'impressions' (conceived of as an interface) played in the traditional account of perception. It is conceived of as entirely 'inside the mind' (or 'inside the head')— a realm where, of course, there are no *deer*—and as connected— causally or mysteriously—with the deer and the meadow 'out there.' *Early modern epistemology and metaphysics saddled us with an interface conception of conception as well as an interface*

65

conception of perception. And, once again, Cartesianism cum materialism has simply retained the interface while identifying it with something in the brain; current talk of 'mental representations' in 'cognitive science' represents just this conception (1999, 45).

Putnam's main argument for the persistence of the interface epistemology or the *'Cartesian cum materialist* epistemology' is its conception of the mind 'as a kind of organ' (1999, 10) placed in the head and thus removed from the world from the very beginning. In fact, this 'mind as an organ' view is also responsible for the celebrated centrality that the topic of realism enjoys in philosophical discussion. Because, if you tuck the mind away from the world right from the beginning then obviously the question that becomes exceedingly pressing is, 'how does the mind hook on to the world?'

What does it mean to think of the mind 'as an organ'? We ordinarily take an organ to be situated in a place and thus to be a thing capable of interacting with its environment, i.e., things outside of it, only *causally.* Take for example, the eye. An eye interacts causally with its environment in the sense that it is effected by what goes on around it; is caused to have certain images etc. Through these affectations only an eye knows its surroundings. Thus an organ does not have any ability to *know* its environment directly. Now applying this idea to the case of mind, Putnam writes,

> If one assumes that the mind is an *organ,* and one goes on to identify the mind with the brain, it will then become irresistible to (1) think of some of the 'representations' as analogous to the classical theorist's 'impressions' and (2) to think that those 'representations' are linked to objects in the organism's environment only causally and not cognitively (1999, 9 -10).

Now what does it mean to interact with something *cognitively?* Putnam would argue that this has to do with the ability to know something directly and not through a screen or an interface. The way to go beyond this is to reject this interface epistemology for a direct theory of perception where the cognitive powers of the mind go all the way to the objects themselves. Putnam wants to replace this 'mind as an organ' view with a view that conceives of mind in terms of abilities that include our abilities of representing, imagining, conceiving etc., and considers 'thoughts as exercises of our object-involving abilities' (Putnam, 1994c, 306). Applying this to the case of realism, what we get is a kind of 'direct realism' or what James called the 'natural realism of the common man' where we are directly involved with things in the world.

Before we move on to outlining Putnam's natural realism, it is important to clarify that to reject the 'Cartesianism cum materialism' is not to revert back to Cartesian dualism. Putnam acknowledges that our cognitive abilities "depend upon our brains and upon all the various transactions between the environment and the organism" (1999, 44). What he is arguing against is the popular urge that these abilities "have to be reductively explained [by] using the vocabulary of physics and biology, or even the vocabulary of computer science" (1999, 44).

Natural Realism: An Outline

Recall, internal realism represents Putnam's initial attempt to overcome what seemed like the insoluble problem of realism. In his reexamination of the conception of mind that serves as the background for this problem Putnam comes to see where his internal realism 'went astray'. His internal realist solution fails because it tried to solve the problem by 'simply pasting together' elements from the two alternatives available. As he writes,

But while the need for a 'third way' besides early modern realism and Dummettian idealism [and Rortian relativism] is something I feel as strongly as ever, such a third way must, as McDowell has repeatedly urged, *undercut* the idea that there is an antinomy and not simply paste together elements of early modern realism and elements of the idealist picture. No conception that retains anything like the traditional notion of sense data [impressions or ideas as interface] can provide a way out; such a conception must always, in the end, leave us confronted by what looks like an insoluble problem (1999, 18).

Putnam's alternative of natural realism instead involves "insisting that 'external things, cabbages and kings, can be *experienced* (And not just in the Pickwickian sense of causing 'experiences,' conceived as affectations of our subjectivity, ...)" (Putnam, 1999, 20) and of course known. And that this can happen directly. This realism is thus characterized by what Putnam calls the 'second naivete' (following J. L. Austin's first naivete) according to which we have unmediated cognitive access to the world. The subtle changes that characterize Putnam's natural realism can be revealed if we carefully look at his discussion on truth.

On Truth

Putnam's turn to natural realism, as we noted above, comes about when he realizes how internal realism fails to be a viable third alternative. In a similar vein, Putnam comes to realize how the metaphysical realist view of truth, and its only apparent possible alternative, the 'deflationist' view of truth rely on the same presupposition. The basic presupposition is that either you take truth to be a 'substantive property' or you take it to be a 'deflationist' property which reduces truth to be a mere matter of speaking.

When philosophers argue that truth is a 'substantial property' what they mean is that there is some property that all and only true sentences have. A metaphysical realist wants "Truth to be something that *goes beyond* the content of the claim and to be that in virtue of which the claim is true" (Putnam, 1999, 55). The result is a 'non-epistemic' or 'recognition-transcendent' notion of truth.

But as we noted, while discussing Putnam's criticism of metaphysical realism, the 'non-epistemic' notion of truth ultimately relies on the world's magical power through which the world identifies the 'intended' reference and correspondence relations for our language (1999, 49). If you do not believe in this 'magical' view, then your only apparent alternative seems to be to embrace a kind of deflationism which takes truth to be a mere matter of speaking. To say, "grass is green' is true", for a deflationist, is just to assert 'grass is green'.

Even in his internal realist period Putnam struggled with this problem as embodying a 'false dilemma'[2] and he came ultimately to characterize truth as 'idealized justification'. He also identifies 'being true' 'with being verified to a sufficient degree to warrant acceptance under sufficiently good epistemic conditions' (Putnam, 1999, 17). What was realistic about this notion of truth, as Putnam had clarified, was that the idea of 'sufficiently good epistemic conditions' was not dependent on our individual or collective ability to verify and/or assert a sentence at a given moment. Putnam also argued that what makes this position on truth 'internal' was the incorporation of conceptual relativity. It thus seems to avoid the metaphysical realist's problem.

However, as Putnam realizes in developing natural realism, the problem lingered just under the surface. Putnam still had to answer how is it possible that we have referential access to 'sufficiently good epistemic conditions'? (1999, 18) It seemed as though the world was still doing the job of fixing this referential relation for us.

These two alternatives seem to be the only possible options once we buy into the interface epistemology described above. If we make room for interface entities like representations in the head, then the pressing question becomes how our knowledge claims involving these representations turn out to be true. Further, if one is not ready to accept the story of the world's magical powers, then it seems as though making a claim of truth necessarily becomes a mere way of speaking. However, we need to be careful about what it is that Putnam rejects while rejecting the interface epistemology.

Putnam clarifies that though there are no representations in the head, there is a sense in which 'representation' is still alive. This is due to the ability that we have to use language, Rorty notwithstanding, to *represent* the world, directly and not through causal entities like representations. And this ability to represent, Putnam remarks, is 'an activity in which we all engage' (1999, 59). To deny this would be to become a victim of the same 'false dilemma' that vitiates metaphysical realism and Rortian relativism.

Using this reading of representation, Putnam wants to find an alternative to the metaphysical realist's way of thinking of truth as a 'substantial property'. However, he wants to make it clear that his aim is to avoid another false dilemma that would force a swing to a deflationary alternative where truth loses all its normativity and becomes a mere matter of speechmaking. "The right alternative," Putnam writes,

> is to recognize that empirical statements already make claims about the world—many different sorts of claims about the world—whether or not they contain the words *is true*. What is wrong in deflationism is that it cannot properly accommodate the truism that certain claims about the world are (not merely assertable or verifiable but) *true* (1999, 55 -56).

Following Wittgenstein, Putnam identifies the problem underlying the false dilemma as an eagerness to specify one single property that all true statements need to share. Replacing this conception of truth as a 'freestanding property', Putnam, in a Wittgensteinian spirit, asks us to look for truth in our uses, in our different kinds of discourses, in our various representations of the world. As he explains,

> If Wittgenstein was right, how should his reflections affect our view of the concept of truth? On the one hand, to regard an assertion or a belief or a thought as true or false *is* to regard it as being right or wrong; on the other hand, just what sort of

rightness or wrongness is in question varies enormously with the *sort* of discourse. *Statement, true, refers,* indeed, *belief, assertion, thought, language* – all the terms we use when we think about logic (or 'grammar') in the wide sense in which Wittgenstein understands that notion – have a plurality of uses, and new uses are constantly added as new forms of discourse come into existence. On the other hand, that does not mean that any practices at all of employing 'marks and noises' can be recognized by us as adding up to a form of discourse – for not every way of producing marks and noises is 'one in which there is the face of meaning at all' (1999, 69).

Putnam further notes, "the rich and ever-growing collection of truths about the world ... is the product of the world, with language users playing a creative role in the process of production" (1994b, 265).

Generalizing this view on truth to the issue of realism he writes,

> The notion that our words and life are constrained by a reality not of our own invention plays a deep role in our lives and is to be respected. The source of the puzzlement lies in the common philosophical error of supposing that the term *reality* must refer to a single superthing instead of looking at the ways in which we endlessly renegotiate—and are *forced* to renegotiate—our notion of reality as our language and our life develop (1999, 9).

Putnam's Three Realisms: Compared and Contrasted

I have discussed three kinds of realism that Putnam has subscribed to at different points in his philosophical journey, namely, metaphysical realism, internal realism and natural realism. Among these three, internal realism and natural realism are closer to each other because they are both the result of Putnam's attempts to find a middle ground between 'reactionary metaphysics and irresponsible relativism'. However, an interesting interrelation between these three realisms emerges when we consider how they interpret the idea of mind-dependence (or independence) of the world.

In metaphysical realism our language 'mirrors' the world by providing different descriptions of the mind-independent reality. The world is taken to have its own inherent language or structure and the job of a philosopher is to 'discover' this language. The descriptions that such attempted 'discoveries' produce amount to mere copies. The main theme of internal realism, you will recall, is one where 'the mind and the world together create the mind and the world'. This leaves the impression that the world is, in some sense, dependent on or created by the mind. What characterizes Putnam's move to natural realism is his uneasiness about the talk of 'mind dependence'. He writes, "I regret having myself spoken of 'mind dependence' in connection with these issues ..." (1994a, 448). What happens in this period is that the alternative portrayal of the mind either as creating the world or as copying the world is given up. This is because the whole idea of the mind as a thing approaching the world which is another thing is also rejected. The mind is not a thing upon which the world is dependent or independent. There is only one thing, namely, the world which includes various things including our cognitive abilities and of course our brains upon which those abilities depend. In the natural realism period our world is of course mind-independent, but only in a very naïve and innocent sense. As Putnam writes,

> The traditional metaphysician is perfectly right to insist on the independence of reality and our cognitive responsibility to do justice to whatever we describe; but the traditional picture of a reality that dictates the totality of possible descriptions once and for all preserves *those* insights at the cost of losing the *real* insight in James's pragmatism, the insight that 'description' is never a mere copying and that we constantly add to the ways in which language can be responsible to reality. And this is the insight we must not throw away in our haste to recoil from James's unwise talk of our (partly) 'making up' the world (1999, 8).

In retaining this insight, Putnam argues, we retain the 'spirit of Aristotle's defense of the commonsense world'. Further, the abandonment of the interface epistemology results in, as Putnam writes, in an 'increasingly realist' picture which is liberating and definitely more secure. This also represents the culmination of the increasingly pragmatist spirit in the evolution of Putnam's realism.

Endnotes

[1] Though Putnam uses different names like 'naïve realism', 'direct realism', 'common sense realism' and 'natural realism' etc. in his *Dewey Lectures* and other publications to characterize his views at

this stage, I have only used the name 'natural realism' to avoid confusion.

[2] One commits the fallacy of false dilemma when one assumes that there are only two possibilities when there are more than two.

6

On Philosophy of Mathematics, Physics and Logic

"As the circle of science grows larger, it touches paradox at more places." *Indeed*! Quantum mechanics is a beautiful example of the way in which increased understanding can make the world a more paradoxical place.
    -- Hilary Putnam, "Realism with a Human Face"

Mathematics is not an experimental science; that is the first thing that every philosopher learns. Yet the adoption of the axiom of choice as a new mathematical paradigm *was* an experiment, even if the experiment was not performed by men in white coats in a laboratory.
    -- Hilary Putnam, "Science as Approximation to Truth"

Introduction

Putnam's entry into philosophy began with his Ph. D. dissertation[1] in the philosophy of physics written under the supervision of the famous philosopher of physics, Hans Reichenbach. In his early years as a philosopher Putnam focused much of his attention on problems from philosophy of mathematics, physics and logic.

In the realm of mathematics and mathematical logic, his principal contribution consists of solving 'Hilbert's 10ᵗʰ Problem' (with Martin Davis and Julia Robinson) "by showing the unsolvability of the decision problem for exponential Diophantine equations" (Putnam, 1990, 253). In the field of philosophy of physics his main contribution consists of providing an interesting way of understanding the scientific revolution that resulted from the theory of relativity and quantum mechanics. To discuss the exact nature of these contributions would require a sophisticated mastery of advanced mathematics and physics that is beyond the scope of this book. What would be useful for our purposes is to explain the basic problems that Putnam tries to address in these fields and also the main course of development of his views in relation to these problems. As will become evident, this development not only reflects Putnam's journey from metaphysical realism to his current position of natural realism but also provides a picture of the problems that necessitated that journey.

Philosophy of Physics

The 'two-slit' Experiment and the 'Schrodinger's cat'

The main topic Putnam focuses on in philosophy of physics is the problem of interpretation of quantum mechanics. More specifically, it is a problem of a *realistic* interpretation of quantum mechanics. The need for this interpretation arises since in quantum mechanics the position of a particle can be uncertain. We can explain this problem with the help of the celebrated 'two-slit experiments'.

Let us imagine a device consisting of two screens placed one in front of the other, the first with two fine slits and the second equipped with a photographic emulsion designed to respond to the impact of a particle. Now imagine a point source that releases a beam of particles (of photons or electrons) that passes through the screen with two slits and is then detected on the emulsion of the second screen as it emerges from the first screen. Imagine further that we control the speed of the beams such that on average only one particle is passing through this device at a given time. Here is how the uncertainty of the position of the particle, in this case a photon, plays out:

> The uncertainty in the position of the photon permits *each* photon to interact with *both* slits, so that what one gets on the photographic plate is not a simple sum of the patterns that one would obtain by just performing the experiment with the left slit open and just performing the experiment with the right slit open. Rather, it is as if *half* the photon went through the left hand slit and *half* the photon went through the right hand slit and the two halves then intermingled and interfered .... [This feature is also called the 'superposition of states'.] The final result is a system of visible interference fringes in the photographic picture. Yet, in spite of all this wave-like behavior, *each individual photon strikes the emulsion at one and only one definite point.* We never succeed in *demonstrating* that the photon is physically

74

'smeared out' by getting it to hit the emulsion in a way that leaves a smeared out crater or other proof that something spatially extended struck; it is only that the interference fringes force us to *infer* that the photon was spatially spread out *when we were not interacting with it* (Putnam, 1983, 47- 8).

Thus the problem seems to be that the same particle exhibits what is classically called, a wave-like behavior in its passage through the first screen with the slits, but particle-like behavior in respect to its detection at the second screen. To use Putnam's helpful imagery to explain this phenomenon:

> It is like the Charles Addams cartoon of the skiier who is skiing down a hill, and whose tracks pass on opposite sides of a large tree. We do not *see* the skiier pass through a tree – we have never seen such a thing, nor will we ever – but the tracks seem to force the inference that the skiier passed through the tree before we looked (1983, 48).

The call for interpretation is captured in the following question: "...how can an electron [or a photon] behave both like a wave *and* like a particle?" (Redhead,[2] 1994, 161)

This paradox that emerges for a realist is, how best to capture this wave-like behavior of the particle which clearly seems to defy basic laws of classical logic? According to classical logic, a particle going through the first screen (with the slits) can only be at one of the two possible locations, namely, slit A *or* slit B. But the wave-like behavior, which makes it seem as though half of the particle is at slit A while the other half is at slit B, makes it hard for a realist to represent the position of the particle when it is going through the screen with slits.

Notice also that the uncertainty here is not a mere matter of ignorance on our part about where the particle is. The problem of interpretation arises from the fact that we *cannot* know where the particle is since the particle seems to be 'smeared out over its possible locations'. In other words, the position of the particle *is* uncertain and the challenge for a realist is to show how this wave-like behavior represents *real* behavior and not just mere mathematical probabilities.

To appreciate the dramatic thrust of the challenge facing a realist, we have to consider the phenomenon called the 'collapse' or the 'reduction of the wave packet' (Putnam, 1975a, 134) which characterizes what happens to a particle which is in a 'superposition of different states', when a measurement is done. When this measurement is made the particle 'jumps' indeterministically into a state with a definite value. The strangeness of quantum mechanics consists of the fact that it seems as though the state of the particle is not just uncertain, it is actually in an indeterminate physical state. Indeed, the particle then remains in this indeterminate (probabilistic) state until it is observed. Let me explain this with the famous example of 'Schrodinger's cat'.

The scenario in 'Schrodinger's cat', taken from physicist Erwin Schrodinger, is similar in important respects to the 'two-slit' case. Imagine a cat in an isolated system. At a predetermined time t_0, a particle is released from a source and strikes a half-silvered mirror. There are two possibilities following this strike. Either the particle passes through the mirror and strikes a detector that activates an equipment that kills the cat; or the particle is reflected by the mirror and the cat is not killed. The state that the cat will be in after the time t_0 is the 'unimaginable state of being in a superposition' of being killed and not being killed. However, when an observer looks to see what happened, the 'superposition' of different states 'collapses' and the cat 'jumps' into a definite state of being alive or being dead.

The challenge that this phenomenon presents to a classical realist – one who accepts the classical laws of logic – is that a realist has to be able to explain how the unobserved state (during the 'superposition') and observed states of the cat can be conjoined. This conjunction has to be possible since classical logic tells us that we can introduce a conjunction between any two states of a system. Further, if our realist accepts the law of non-contradiction, quantum mechanics appears to allow that something can be a living cat and a non-living cat (a dead cat!) at the same time.

Putnam's Solutions to the Interpretation Problem

In his first solution Putnam (1957) agreed with Riechenbach that one needs a three-valued logic[3] to solve this puzzle. In this solution we can treat (AvB), i.e., particle is either in slit A or particle is either in slit B, as meaningful, but to avoid 'causal anomalies' (mysterious non-local action by the particle as it goes through the screen with slits), we must regard (AvB) as neither true nor false but accord it a third truth-value, namely, indeterminate. But Putnam later (1965) came to abandon this position as *ad hoc*. As he writes,

> In Reichenbach's approach, for example, it is simply assumed that statements about macro-observables have the conventional two truth values while statements about micro-observables may have a third truth value; but this radical dichotomy between

macro- and micro-observables is not derived from anything, but simply built into the theory *ad hoc* (1975a, 83).

In this period Putnam came to think that "there is *no* satisfying [realist] interpretation of this problem [of interpretation]" (Putnam, 1975a, 157). In 1969, drawing on the ideas of von Neumann, Putnam argued that a bivalent but non-distributive logic – a logic that accepts only two possible values, namely, True and False but restricts the law of distribution[4] to non-superposition states – can serve as a resource for a realist in removing the paradox associated with the interpretation of quantum mechanics.[5] This idea later develops into quantum logic.

However as he entered his internal realist phase he realizes that mere quantum logic is not enough to solve the realist interpretation problem. What one needs to make room for is the 'perspectivalism' that von Neumann's interpretation of quantum mechanics[6] presents. This is because quantum mechanics seems to suggest that there is a 'cut between the system and the observer' (i.e., between the unobserved phenomenon and the observed value), and that there is no way to know the system without approaching it from a particular perspective of an observer. According to the internal realist solution, what helps fill the gap between the unobserved phenomenon and the observed value is a conceptual scheme, which in this case is the observer's perspective. As Putnam writes,

> Although the interpretation I have proposed is not realistic in the sense of assuming a copy theory of truth (metaphysical realism), or even in the sense of assuming that all observables have determinate values, it is *internally* realistic in the sense that *within the interpretation* no distinction appears between 'measured values' and 'unmeasured values'. ... micro-entities spoken of in quantum mechanics are as 'real' as any entities knowable by us, ... There are real entities; *but which they are is relative to the observer* (1983, 269).

However, as Putnam notes in his "Comments and Replies" in *Reading Putnam* (1994b), he finally comes to abandon this internal realist defense since he realizes that the presuppositions underlying perspectivalism and quantum logic turn out to be inconsistent.[7]

Philosophy of Mathematics and Logic

The main themes that Putnam deals with in philosophy of mathematics and logic are the possibility of 'logicism' – a movement that tries to reduce mathematics to logic, and the status of the laws of logic. Putnam's general views in the philosophy of mathematics have gone through similar shifts like his views in the philosophy of physics. However, his first and foremost goal in mathematics was to question mathematical foundationalism – the idea that mathematics provides a foundation for the rest of the sciences.

Dissatisfaction with foundationalism characterizes all the stages through which Putnam's philosophy has evolved. In the initial stage, of metaphysical realism, he argues against foundationalism from two directions. From one direction he argues that mathematics is an empirical or quasi-empirical science while from the other direction he argues that even the laws of logic, which are supposed to protect the a priori foundational nature of mathematics, can be revised. In the later stage of natural realism, his criticism of foundationalism grows out of the fact that the very question regarding the revisable and a priori status of the laws of logic fails to make any sense.

Logicism

'Logicism' is a movement given birth by Frege and made philosophically popular by Russell and Whitehead in the early part of the twentieth century. The main objective of this movement was to reduce mathematics to logic and thereby prove that 'mathematics is logic in disguise' and '*that* is what accounts for its [mathematics'] certainty' (Putnam, 1994c, 499). The motivation was to provide a foundation for mathematics in logic. The received view about the foundation of mathematics was that it consists of a body of a few necessary truths (typically axioms) that are taken to be unrevisably true, i.e., true for ever, and that it provides the foundation for the rest of mathematics as well as other empirical sciences.

However, with the development of non-Euclidean geometry, which showed that axioms of a mathematical discipline need not be necessarily true, the need to find a foundation for mathematics was renewed. When one assumes that mathematics is different from all other empirical sciences, in being foundational to them, the advent of non-Euclidean geometry naturally brings about a sense of 'crisis in the foundation' for all the sciences. Logicism's response to this 'crisis' was to safeguard mathematical necessity by reducing mathematics to logic. Putnam's first attack against logicism is contained in his argument that mathematics is after all empirical. His second argument consists of his challenging the unrevisable and necessary character ascribed to the laws of logic.

Mathematics is Empirical

One of the chief characteristics of an empirical science is that 'for each theory there are usually alternatives in the field, or at least alternatives struggling to be born' (Putnam, 1975a, 51). What makes mathematics seem different from all these sciences is the fact that there usually are no alternatives in the field. Putnam concedes that mathematics is not exactly like other empirical sciences because 'major parts of classical logic and number theory and analysis have no alternatives in the filed' (Putnam, 1975a, 51). But under the above characterization of empirical science, in terms of the possible alternative hypotheses, mathematics does become empirical in the sense that one is *allowed* to try to put alternatives into the field.

Further, mathematics is more like the empirical sciences than generally acknowledged since it strives to discover the truth just as any other empirical sciences. Putnam concludes by noting that what these empirical and quasi-empirical features of mathematics point out is that the 'foundational' view of mathematical knowledge is as suspect as the foundational view of empirical knowledge. Since empirical foundationalism no longer finds serious advocates, mathematical foundationalism is bound to suffer a similar fate. From this it seemed evident that the entire research agenda of 'logicism' was ill-conceived. Putnam identifies the direction in which he would want us to move:

[it is] the direction of making the knowledge of mathematical truth dependent upon experience. If we move further in that direction by recognizing that mathematical methodology involves quasi-empirical elements, and by recognizing that the existence of mathematical objects is representation-relative, then I believe we get a better approximation to the truth (1975a, xii).

Status of the Laws of Logic

One of the assumptions that made the logicist project attractive is the faith many had that laws of logic are unrevisable and necessarily true. Consequently, it was believed that laws of logic were capable of providing the much-required foundation for mathematics. But are logical laws really necessary?

Putnam's position on this question has undergone an important and interesting shift. While arguing against Reichenbachean (in physics) and Carnapean (in mathematics) linguistic conventionalism,[8] he agreed with Quine that all the laws of logic including the logical and mathematical truths are revisable and therefore not fit to shoulder the weight of being analytic, a priori and necessary truths. Rather, they are synthetic. Let us briefly recount Putnam's argument.

Logical positivism holds that mathematical and logical truths are true simply by virtue of the 'rules of language'. But this account runs into trouble if we further take these rules of language to be conventional in nature (i.e., conventionally determined by stipulation). Let us ask what we mean when we speak of something being 'true by convention'. If we mean that mathematical and logical truths are *individually* made true by convention' then a problem arises. This is because given that mathematical and logical truths are infinite, and our acts of stipulation are only finite, these acts cannot make an infinite number of things true. So the claim, 'logical truths are true by convention', 'can only mean that they *follow* from convention'. That is to say, they are true in the sense of "being *logical consequences* of conventions. But the use of the notion of *logical consequence* makes such an account of logical truth viciously circular" (Putnam, 1994c, 500).

Further, if this model of convention is replaced by a 'model of practice' of 'holding certain truths absolutely immune from revision' (Putnam, 1994c, 500-1), then it fails to take into account the fact that

> the *observation that a calculation actually has a certain result* has a kind of 'brute fact' character which enables it, in certain circumstances, to overthrow even the best entrenched general principle. The fact is that there is a certain 'synthetic' element in at least *combinatorial* mathematics, and it is the failure of 'rule of language' accounts to acknowledge this that ultimately makes them simply unbelievable (Putnam, 1994c, 501).

This realization leads Putnam (1962) to agree with Quine that every truth is revisable because there are circumstances under which it would be rational to accept its denial. However, in "There is at least one a priori truth" (in 1983) Putnam distances himself from Quine and argues that there is at least one a priori (unrevisable) truth in logic, namely, 'the minimal principle of contradiction' that 'not every sentence is both true and false'. He argues that since there seems to be no circumstances under which it seems rational to give up this principle, this principle supplies us with at least one a priori truth that is absolutely and unconditionally true. He concludes this essay with the following words:

> the laws of logic are so central to our thinking that they define what a rational argument is. This may not show that we could never change our mind about the laws of logic, i.e., that no

causal process could lead us to vocalize or believe different statements; but it does show that we could not be brought to change our minds by a rational argument ... [The laws of logic] are presupposed by so much of the activity of argument that it is no wonder that we cannot envisage their being overthrown ... by rational argument (1983, 107).

In "Rethinking Mathematical Necessity" (in 1990) Putnam goes forward to alter this position in turn. He is still opposed to the view he once held with Quine, namely that laws of logic are simple empirical truths. But what he changes in this essay is *how* he wants to criticize and distance himself from this view. Instead of attacking that view by offering an alternative, he now raises doubt about the very nature of the question, namely, whether the laws of logic are revisable or a priori. He now wants to argue that this question is 'one which we are unable to make any clear sense of'.

In this relation he offers an example in the form of a riddle: "A court lady once fell into disfavor with the king. The king, intending to give her a command impossible of fulfillment, told her to come to the Royal Ball 'neither naked nor dressed'" (1994c, 254). The clever lady's solution was to appear 'in a fishnet'. Putnam now wants to compare this riddle with the philosophical question that asks about the revisability of the laws of logic and remarks:

> Concerning such riddles, Wittgenstein says that we are able to give them a sense only after we know the solution; the solution bestows a sense on the riddle-question. This seems right [for the philosophical question concerning the revisability of the laws of logic] (1994c, 254).

Thus in rejecting the Carnapean alternative of linguistic conventionalism (that rendered these truths as analytic) and the Quinean alternative of non-apriorism (that rendered these truths as purely empirical and synthetic), Putnam also rejects the question of mathematical foundationalism.

Summary and Conclusion

Given the technical nature of the issues discussed in this chapter and the number of different views that Putnam takes on these issues, a summary section seems pertinent. This summary will also give us an opportunity to note how Putnam's changing views in these areas reflect the evolution that his general philosophical outlook has undergone. Let us start with the philosophy of mathematics.

In Putnam's writing in this area, we can detect three stages through which his ideas have evolved. The first phase is dominated by a non-positivist and non-verificationist frame of mind that holds a position similar to Quine's revisability thesis and the rejection of the a priori. The second phase represents his distancing himself from Quine and the final phase represents a real transition since in surpassing the options presented in phase one and phase two, Putnam here offers a new outlook on the nature of the questions as well as the underlying presuppositions.

These three stages reflect the three realist positions that Putnam has held, namely, metaphysical realism, internal realism and common sense or natural realism. Metaphysical realism seems to be the natural choice in the first stage since the main goal here is to 'do philosophy of physics and mathematics from a realist perspective' and the only realism that seemed available to Putnam was metaphysical realism. Since the aim is to arrive at *the* true picture of the mind-independent world, Quine's position of 'no a priorism' (in the sense of no unrevisability) seems correct.

In the internal realism phase the hypothesis of realism gets subsumed under a language or a conceptual scheme. Putnam comes to realize that true claims can only be made from the perspective of a given language. Naturally in mathematics this leads him to argue that at least some truths of mathematics and logic are true a priori and not revisable. These truths give us the standards of rationality.

We have noted in our previous chapter that Putnam's natural realism is a result of reevaluation and rejection of a few assumptions that underlie his early writings. In the field of mathematics this motivates him to examine the very nature of the question regarding the revisability of the laws of logic and to withhold from proposing a new alternative.

In the realm of the philosophy of physics we can trace a similar evolution. His initial solution to the interpretation problem of quantum mechanics, you will recall, was either to take refuse in three-valued logic or to introduce a quantum logic that relied on Quine's idea that even the laws of logic can be revised. This too is clearly motivated by metaphysical realist intuitions since the aim here is to 'mirror' the mind-independent world of quantum mechanics by fixing one's logic.

The internal realism phase leads him to embrace perspectivalism in the realm of quantum mechanics that solves the problem of interpretation by taking the observer's perspective in arriving at the measurement of the particle's position rather than a perspective 'from nowhere'. Finally, the naïve realism phase persuades him to reexamine the consistency of the assumptions behind perspectivalism. Once again what we have here is a gradual evolution of ideas that changes its course in response to the emerging problems while remaining at its core an attempt to do philosophy from a realist point of view.

Endnotes

[1] This dissertation titled "The Meaning of the Concept of Probability in Application to Finite Sequences" is published in 1990 by Garland Publishers with an "Introduction Some Years Later".

[2] This piece of Redhead presents a very sophisticated and detailed exposition of Putnam's positions on quantum logic and quantum mechanics.

[3] In a three-valued logic, a particle's position can have one of three possible values, namely, True, False and Indeterminate.

[4] The law of distribution is a method of conjunction introduction. For example, from [p v (q&r)], classical logic allows you to arrive at [(pvq) & (pvr)] by the law of distribution.

[5] Explaining how he solves this problem would require us to understand quantum logic and quite a bit of mathematics. Given the focus of this book, I am not going to try to explain these things. See Putnam's "Quantum Mechanics and the Observer" and his "Possibility and Necessity" (both reprinted in Putnam 1983) and Part I of "Realism with a Human Face" (in Putnam, 1990) for a detailed treatment of this.

[6] Von Neumann's perspectivalism does not really rely on the ideas that Putnam developed into quantum logic, though they both predict the same phenomenon.

[7] Once again I have not ventured to explain how this comes about. Interested readers can go to Putnam (1994b, 273-279).

[8] This conventionalism is the view that truths are true by convention' or by the 'rules of language'. It falls quite nicely out of an eagerness to rescue and defend the logical positivist distinction between the analytic and the synthetic.

7

On Moral and Social Matters

Metaphysics without Ethics is blind.
-- Hilary Putnam, *Meaning and the Moral Sciences*

Introduction

Putnam's ideas on moral and political issues center on the distinction between fact and value, or as it has been ceremoniously called, 'the fact-value dichotomy'. This focus grows out of his dissatisfaction with positivist scientism as well as his admiration for the pragmatist tradition's emphasis on *how to live*.

In order to appreciate the real thrust of Putnam's moral point of view and the role it plays in the formation of Putnam's main philosophical themes, we need to outline the gradual development of Putnam's moral thought. It is interesting to note that discussions of moral issues have come to occupy the center stage of Putnam's philosophical concern only later, i.e., after his shift to internal realism. Though in a few places in his earlier writings Putnam does question the viability of drawing a sharp distinction between science and morality (or between scientific knowledge and moral knowledge), it is not until after the development of internal realism, that this topic comes to the forefront in his philosophical concerns.

As James Conant has pointed out, this shift exhibits Putnam's realization that the dichotomy between fact and value is a product of our metaphysical confusion about a mind-independent, concept-independent world. So the intuitions that force Putnam to question the viability of metaphysical realism in favor of internal realism are the same intuitions that motivate him to question the fact-value dichotomy.

Further, the realization of the bankruptcy of philosophers' 'craving for objectivity' paves the way for more attention to the moral and social issues. In this regard, Putnam's increased interest in moral and socio-political topics can also be represented as a reflection of his renewed appreciation for Kant's insistence on the 'twin inspiration for philosophy', namely, argument and vision or as Conant puts it 'rigor and human relevance' (in Putnam, 1990, xxxii).

While rejecting the 'fact-value' dichotomy, Putnam will note that this distinction was developed to devalue moral judgements in the sense that there can be no way of differentiating between better and worse judgments. Rejecting this dichotomy is not, however, to accept a kind of moral realism in the sense that there can be absolute truths about moral matters that can be discovered from the 'God's eye view'. Rather, extending the spirit of internal realism to the moral realm, Putnam will argue that moral judgments can only be made within a conceptual scheme or what he calls a 'moral image of the world'. Further, within each 'moral image' we can differentiate between better and worse or right and wrong judgments.

The fact-value dichotomy

Those who want to draw the distinction between facts and values[1] would ask you to consider the following pair of claims: (A): New York state is on the east coast of the United States; (B): Abortion is wrong, or One should take care of one's parents in their old age. This person would then draw your attention to the fact that while certain kinds of questions can be asked about (A), no such questions can be raised about (B). More specifically, while we can ask whether (A) is true or false and we would know how to determine the answer (i.e., by looking at a reliable US map), it does not make sense to ask whether (B) is true or false.

An even clearer distinction between fact and value falls out of the positivist verificationist principle of meaning. According to this principle, the meaning of a sentence is given in its method of verification. A sentence, thus, has meaning (or 'cognitive significance') when we can tell how (by what means or by means of what kinds of observations, experiments etc.) to verify that sentence or to determine whether that sentence is true or false. A corollary of this claim is that to have cognitive significance or cognitive meaning is to have a truth-value. To lack cognitive significance, conversely, is to lack a truth-value.

Now the question is, what happens when we apply the verificationist principle of meaning to our value judgments, i.e., judgments that involve concepts like good or bad, right or wrong, ought or should etc. (Statement (B) above)? Since we don't know how to verify these judgments, or what kinds of situations would help us determine whether such a statement is true or false, these judgments turn out to lack any truth-value and in turn, lack cognitive significance. This view is generally called the non-cognitivism about ethics.

Non-cognitivism can take various forms like emotivism, prescriptivism etc. Emotivism is the view that the sole significance or purpose of moral discourse is to express feelings, attitudes, broadly emotions. Prescriptivism, on the other hand, contends that the sole significance of moral discourse lies in its ability to express moral prescriptions.

Putnam's Criticism of the Fact-Value Dichotomy

The main characteristic of this dichotomy is that facts are inherently different from values. While facts are objective, non-controversial, mind-independent and concept-independent, values are subjective, controversial, mind-dependent, and above all, according to cultural relativism, dependent on cultural norms of a community. However, ethical non-cognitivism is by no means a view without problems.

The main source of non-cognitivism's problems is largely the same as the problems facing the verificationist principle. One of the presuppositions behind the verification principle is that one can identify the verification conditions for each sentence *individually* and further that one can also test independently whether these conditions obtain in a particular case. This supposition ties into accepting the analytic-synthetic distinction. According to this distinction while some of our sentences (namely, the analytic ones like 'a bachelor is an unmarried man') are true purely by meaning, others (the synthetic ones like 'snow is white') are not. However, as Quine (1951) points out, this distinction for all its (a priori) reasonableness, simply has not been drawn. And Quine and others see virtually no hope for doing so on the horizon. The result for Quine is a shift to holism where 'Our statements face the tribunal of experience as a whole and not individually'.

Further, as it turned out, many statements of the hard sciences (especially the theoretical claims) would lose their cognitive significance under this principle because it would be very hard, if not impossible, to determine what their verification conditions would consist in. Finally, this positivist principle turns out to be self-refuting because the very statement that expresses this principle turns out to be non-verifiable itself. Given these troubles, one would expect that this dichotomy would lose its attraction. However, as Putnam notes, this dichotomy or some of its sophisticated variants still hold their sway over us. This leads him to offer his own criticisms against this dichotomy.

Putnam's strategy is to argue against this dichotomy from two directions. From one direction, he argues that there are objective facts about values. That is to say, factual claims (i.e., claims that are true or false) can be and are often made about our moral realm. He makes this point by noting the inherent inconsistency in the positivist position of emotivism. From the other direction, he argues that our so-called 'facts' are permeated with values. His argument here basically consists of his general argument against metaphysical realism and in favor of internal realism.

Emotivism's Inherent Inconsistency

According to emotivism 'choosing a morality' is *choosing* a way of life. Morality thus becomes a matter of subjective or at best intersubjective choice, which is lacking in objectivity. This, Putnam argues, turns out to be inconsistent with a very basic fact of our moral lives where we worry whether what we are doing is right or wrong.

An implication of emotivism's view that ethical judgments lack objectivity is that there is no better or worse in moral judgments. What this means is that there can be no real reason for preferring one ethical judgment to the other. It is merely a matter of personal choice, taste etc. Now Putnam notes something interesting that happened to him. Some event occurred in his life which made him think very hard about whether he was doing the right thing – not just whether what he was doing answered the interests of his community but whether what he was doing was right or wrong. This predicament forced Putnam to ask: 'if morality is purely a matter of personal choice, then why am I so worried about whether what I am doing is right or wrong?' In other words, if there is no real reason for preferring one ethical judgment to another, there would be no basis for anxiety over making the right moral choice. However, it is a plain fact of experience that we sometimes do worry about moral matters in this way. Thus, emotivism is inconsistent with some basic facts of moral experience.

Further, Putnam argues, to claim that we want to act morally because our instinct drives us to and/or because of social conditioning is to just miss the point. Putnam gives the example of a boy growing up in the very poor parts of Sicily. Say the boy is offered the opportunity to join the mafia where though he will live an immoral life (involving killing etc.), he will be relatively comfortable. His other option is to remain in the poor conditions. Now, Putnam asks, whether what this boy faces is anything like a mere choice of a way of life, in the sense in which we choose an outdoor lifestyle as opposed to a more sedentary one. Say the boy decides to refuse this opportunity, can it be said that he did what he did because he wanted to impress his neighbors or even because of instincts? In this relation Putnam points out that there is something quite naïve in the way some philosophers claim we choose our way of life:

> It is all very fine for comfortable Oxford professors and comfortable French existentialists to wax rhetorical about how one has to 'choose a way of life' and commit oneself to it (even if the commitment is 'absurd,' the existentialists will add). And this rhetoric really impresses people like ourselves, who are reasonably prosperous. But the poor person who makes such a sacrifice makes it precisely because he does not see it that way. Would anyone *really* choose such a life if he thought that *all* it was was 'a choice of a way of life'? Of course, he makes the choice he does because he knows that that choice is his *duty*. And he knows that he cannot choose his duties, at least not in this respect (1990, 150).

If we deny objectivity of values and thus take reason (rationality) out of morality, what we get for our ethical account is results that are inconsistent with our own moral experience and an ultimate emptiness that lacks any real resources to explain why we all, at least sometimes, worry, whether what one is doing is right or wrong. The problem for Putnam, however, is to incorporate objectivity within our 'soft' realm of morality. We will get to Putnam's answer shortly. But before that let us consider Putnam's argument that our so-called 'hard' facts are permeated by values as well.

How hard are the facts?

How deep does the attraction for the fact-value dichotomy or some variant of it run in the world of the analytic philosophers? By the 1950s it became clear that the epistemological argument presented for this dichotomy, that draws its blood from the principle of confirmation and also the analytic-synthetic distinction, turns out to be incoherent and self-refuting. However, contemporary philosophers have persisted in the attempt to develop a kind of metaphysical defense of this dichotomy, a defense that draws its blood from the nature of truth. What we see in these philosophers (Putnam gives the example of British philosopher Bernard Williams) is that while they accept that our statements of values can be true or false, they argue that the nature of such truth is quite different from the kind of truth that applies to our statements of truly scientific facts.

Williams, for example, argues that the kind of truth that is involved in our value judgments is the same kind that is involved in our judgments about medium-sized objects, like, 'that table is square'. In both these cases, truth turns out to be 'perspectival' i.e., 'dependent on a perspective'. Thus depending on where you are standing in relation to the table, the table may seem square or rectangular. Similarly, depending on what your moral principles are, an act, say abortion, might seem moral or immoral to you. Contrasting this kind of truth with the kind of truth involved in scientific judgments, Williams argues, truth in the latter case is absolute, i.e., perspective-independent. As examples of this kind of absolute truth Williams refers to statements about the ultimate constituents of the physical world as given to us by advanced sciences like physics.

This distinction is reminiscent of the distinction that Locke drew between primary qualities and secondary qualities, i.e., between properties of things that represent aspects of those things and properties of things that do not capture their own aspects. Locke argued that primary qualities like weight, number etc., are real because they correspond to something in the objects but the secondary qualities are 'projected' in the sense that they don't correspond to anything in the objects but rather are how we the observers are effected by certain properties. A very popular example of Locke's secondary qualities is the idea of color (others include smell, taste etc.). The popular idea, at least philosophically, is that the yellow sunset really does not have anything in it that is yellow; rather it is how some of the properties of the setting sun interact with our senses.

Philosophers like Williams argue that our value judgments are like judgments of color because these value judgments represent how subjects are affected by certain things in their environment. In fact, they are worse than the color judgments since in the case of our judgments of color, our realization of their projective (i.e., subjective) nature does not affect the function that these judgments play in our lives. But a realization of the projective or subjective nature of our value judgments raises a crucial question about the very function of these judgments in our lives.

Putnam argues that this distinction that Williams draws between absolute and non-absolute truths is based on the assumption that the ultimate stuff of the world will be discovered by the sciences and that the statements such sciences make are fully devoid of any trace of any perspectivism or value etc. However, as Quine showed us, in the practice of science, when facts and theories come into conflict, there is no one way to solve those conflicts. Sometimes we modify the theory, sometime the 'facts' and sometimes both. It is also not true that these decisions are based purely on 'observational facts'. This is because sometimes we choose between two theories both of which account for the same set of observational facts. Still we judge one to be better or worse than the other. Often what helps us in making the decision are 'desiderata' such as 'simplicity', 'conservatism', and 'coherence' etc. But as Putnam writes, "part of [his] case is that *coherence* and *simplicity* and the like are themselves *values*" (1990, 138).

What follows from the fact that the practice of mature science seems to involve values? Here is what happens according to Putnam:

> If coherence and simplicity are values, and if we cannot deny without falling into total self-refuting subjectivism that *they* are objective (notwithstanding their 'softness,' the lack of well-defined 'criteria,' and so forth), then the classic argument against the objectivity of ethical values is *totally* undercut. For that argument turned on precisely the 'softness' of ethical values – the lack of noncontroversial 'method,' and so on – and on the alleged 'queerness' of the very notion of an *action guiding fact*. But *all* values are in this boat; if *those* arguments show that ethical values are totally subjective, then cognitive values [like coherence, simplicity etc.] are totally subjective as well. (1990, 140)

Putnam further writes,

> ... if 'values' seem a bit suspect from a narrowly scientific point of view, they have, at the very least, a lot of 'companions in the guilt': justification, coherence, simplicity, reference, truth and so on, all exhibit the *same* problems that goodness and kindness do, from an epistemological point of view. None of them is reducible to physical notions; none of them is governed by syntactically precise rules. Rather than give up all of them, ... --we should recognize that *all* values, including the cognitive ones, derive their authority from our idea of human flourishing and our idea of reason. These two ideas are interconnected: our image of an ideal theoretical intelligence is simply a *part* of our ideal of total human flourishing, and makes no sense wrenched out of the total ideal, as Plato and Aristotle saw (1990, 141).

The main thrust of this argument can be captured in an expression of Walsh whose own expression is an improvisation of Quine's famous expression, "..., if a theory may be black with fact and white with convention, it might well be red with values" (quoted in Putnam, 1990, 164). This also represents an extension of Putnam's argument against metaphysical realism which occurred to him as a result of considering the epistemological implications of that position. Let us just briefly recapitulate what was the problem there: if we believed that the mind merely *copied* the world which had its own structure, then the worry remains always how do we know when we have gotten a correct copy? Thus this opens the room for a self-refuting scepticism at the very heart of this Realist position. Now let us see how this line of argumentation applies to the moral realm.

The people who want to draw the distinction between fact and value seem to argue that while in the realm of facts there is an objective world 'facts' about which can be discovered and copied, no such thing is available in the moral realm. Further, if we are to reject this distinction then we have to maintain that there is an objective world even in the moral realm that our principles of morality discover and copy. Indeed this has been the position maintained by many so-called moral Realists starting of course with Plato. Putnam's main argument against this kind of moral realism is similar to his argument against metaphysical realism: there is no way of telling which picture copies this objective world of morality better than the other. This, however, as the turn to internal realism insisted, is not to embrace a position of 'anything goes'.

What form does the internal realist position take when applied to the moral realm? What is the alternative that Putnam is suggesting? To find out more about this we need to turn to what Putnam calls the *moral image of the world*. Keeping in tune with his 'Kantian' spirit of internal realism, the spirit that a world can only be understood by applying our own set of concepts, Putnam develops his conception of the moral image out of his 'Kantian' criticism of moral realism.

The Moral Image of the World

Putnam's presentation of at least one strand of Kant can be perceived as uncovering the pragmatist streak in Kant's moral thinking. Pragmatism not only stands for a concern with the practice, i.e., how to live, but its most important departure from traditional philosophy is in its insistence that we cannot and need not know the final truth or the absolute truth. In other words, it is in its embracing of human fallibility that pragmatism makes its most important mark. Further, it is this mark that sets pragmatism apart from all other isms. This is because, as becomes clear from Putnam's attack on objectivity and the science/ethics distinction, one of the motivations behind positivism, scientism, scepticism and even Williams' kind of ethical relativism is a certain image about knowledge, namely, that in order to know something we have to be absolutely certain about it.[2] Now how does this point get incorporated in Putnam's reading of Kant and also in Putnam's views on morality?

Let us start with the standard reading of Kant. According to this reading the central moral distinction that Kant draws between autonomy and heteronomy can be captured in the following terms. You are heteronomous when your moral ideals, principles, etc. are given to you from outside, i.e., which are not acquired as a result of your own reflection, your own thinking. Conversely, you are autonomous when you are thinking on your own. But what does it mean to be thinking on your own? Putnam suggests two possible answers.

First, each one of us carries a blue print and when faced with a problem we consult this blue print within us and figure out what one should do (i.e., what end is to be achieved) and how one should achieve it (i.e., the means). In this understanding having reason is like having certain program, so to speak, available to one and having freewill will be like having the ability to consult this program and figure out the outcome. Further, in this understanding having freewill and reason exhausts one's autonomy. Putnam argues that this is the Medieval understanding of free will and reason which treats solving the autonomy and freewill puzzle as similar to solving an 'engineering problem'. In this understanding reason not only gives us the ability to think about morality but also tells us what our moral ends are. So exercising freewill under this interpretation is nothing but finding out or reading the letters on the blue print. Independent thinking in this interpretation goes in so far as figuring out individually the dictates of reason.

The second possibility that Putnam offers does not present such a soothing picture. According to this picture reason does not tell us or determine for us the contents of moral principles. Freedom here consists merely of each one's having the ability to think on one's own. This reading of autonomy accepts that there is a certain problematic about the content of morality. This is because there is no a priori way of determining moral content. But as we will note shortly, Putnam contends that it is this uncertainty and openness that preserves our autonomy. It is this unorthodox reading of Kantian autonomy which Putnam wants to use in explaining his conception of the moral image of the world.

92

Putnam aligns his conception of the moral image alongside Kant's image of the world in the epistemological realm.[3] Kant's way to solve the impasse between the empiricists and the rationalists was to suggest that knowledge proper requires not only input from the external world but also structure from human mind and/or understanding. Applying this to the moral realm, Putnam argues, the so-called elements of the moral world, namely, the moral principles, can not be grasped or understood without bringing in our own categories of understanding. These categories are encapsulated in our 'moral images of the world'. What constitutes our moral image is an interdependent network of moral principles which support each other. Putnam goes on to replace Kant's idea of *the* moral image of the world with different moral images. And he then argues, just as Kant did only in terms of one moral image, that no moral situation can be made sense of without being understood in terms of this or that moral image of the world. This point parallels Putnam's argument that internal realism gives us realism, but only relative to a conceptual scheme. Here, the point is that the concept of a moral image provides objectivity for morality, even if that objectivity is relative to a particular moral image.

Putnam also takes this above position of Kant to further suggest that one cannot differentiate between the input of the world and the input of the human mind or human conception. Rather what we have is an intertwined enterprise. Putnam writes,

> Kant's glory, in my eyes, is to say that the very fact that we cannot separate our own conceptual contribution from what is 'objectively there' is not a disaster. It is, in fact, a certain kind of guarantee; [of our autonomy and dignity]..." (1987, 52).

In Putnam's view, Kant's strategy 'is to *celebrate* the loss of essences, without turning back to Humean empiricism' (1987, 52). However, the worry is, once we tie truth to the interpreter's point of view then are we not going to lose truth altogether? That is to say, can there be any way of differentiating Putnam's position from that of a cultural relativist? But as we have noted in our chapter on internal realism, this is the same question as to the viability of claiming that internal realism is still realism. In the moral realm this question takes the following form. Given that there are different moral images of the world, with their own network of values and moral principles, how can we differentiate between better and worse moral images? In other words, the problem is that if we once open the floodgates of perspectivalism, there will be no objective ground remaining for claiming that one perspective is better than the other; it is going to be a matter of pure taste or preference.

Putnam, in replying to this issue, uses an image used by his wife, and frequent collaborator in his moral and political writings, Ruth Anna Putnam, namely, that of our artefact building. Take for example, our practice of knife building. True, there is no grand plan or blueprint that every knife builder follows. Rather, the very nature of artefact building is such that our purposes, our needs, and broadly speaking, our particular predicament and perspectives are always shaping our interests. But just because there is no objective plan of knife building, Putnam asks, can we say that there is no way of differentiating between better or worse knives? (1987, 78 -79)

Now, if you are thinking that while there are clear criteria that help us differentiate between better and worse knives, there are no such clear criteria available in the moral realm, Putnam would ask you the following question: What makes such criteria available in the case of knife-making? Of course, you would reply, human needs. Putnam would then reply that we human beings have moral needs as well and they in a similar way help us figure out, though not in any a priori fashion, the moral standards that help us differentiate between better and worse moral images. Just as there is no foundation in any other sphere of knowledge, there is no foundation for moral knowledge either. The mistake is in the epistemological image of a final foundation based upon the untenable picture of metaphysical realism. But Putnam's uniqueness lies in his forcing analytic philosophers to see the pragmatist idea that to abandon foundationalism is not the same as holding a position of 'anything goes'. As he writes,

> Once we have given up the picture of a totality of Noumenal Objects and Properties from which our different conceptual schemes merely make one or another selection, the picture of a Noumenal Dough which our conceptual schemes merely 'slice up' differently, we are forced to recognize with William James that the question as to how much of our web of beliefs reflects the world 'in itself' and how much is our 'conceptual contribution' makes no more sense than the question: 'Does a man walk more essentially with his left leg or his right'? *The trail of the human serpent is over all* (1987, 77, emphasis added).

Putnam as a Social Activist

Putnam was the Harvard faculty sponsor of Students for a Democratic Society (SDS) and a member of the Maoist group called the Progressive Labor Party during the Vietnam war. Later his Marxist-Leninism gave way to a form of a liberal socialism. Once again this shift of position reflects the general evolution in his philosophical outlook. This shift reflects his coming to realize that both Marxist-Leninism and capitalism – the view that Marxist-Leninism was responding to and providing an alternative for – share a common presupposition. It is the presupposition that the problems of human political engagements can be solved once and forever. It is this absolutism that Putnam, in a truly pragmatist spirit, attacks throughout his later writings. His life of activism is no different either.

Replacing this craving for infallibility with a spirit that accepts and celebrates the fallibilistic nature of human endeavor, Putnam embraces a liberalism that provides a new sense of human equality. In this respect it is useful to note what Putnam has to say about how *not* to solve moral (and I would add political) problems.

How not to Solve a Moral Problem?

The entire vocabulary of problem and solution carry with itself a tone of finality which in Putnam's opinion reflects our deep-rooted scientism. This vocabulary is misleading since it gives the impression that ethical and political problems can be solved once and for all. But, as Putnam points out, we humans are 'self-surprising' creatures (1995, 32), devoid of any essences. The metaphor that Putnam prefers to apply to the moral and political realm is the 'metaphor of adjudication' (1990, 181) and the 'metaphor of reading or interpreting'. Adjudication differs from a solution in that while the latter is introduced as the 'final (last) word', adjudication does not try to do any such thing. Adjudication, as when the courts adjudicate, involves giving a reasonable decision (verdict) after taking all the relevant facts into account. But there is always the possibility that that verdict may get overturned. Adjudication, as Putnam points out, can nonetheless be better or worse in the sense of being wise or unwise.

In conclusion, a word on Putnam – the philosopher-activist. We have witnessed his public shifts of positions both in philosophical and political realism. However, far from showing a weak-minded thinker what these shifts express is a real spirit of activism that takes a genuine interest in changing the world for better. As he says, while analyzing the state of philosophy and also the role of philosophy in human life,

For Philosophy to see itself simply as thinking about a collection of riddles seems too small an ambition. But for philosophy to have the ambition of saving the world seems too extreme. Something in between has got to be right (1988a, 56).

Endnotes

[1] Hume was the first Western philosopher to draw this distinction. He also argued that evaluative conclusions couldn't be derived from a set of premises that are purely factual and *vice versa*. An attempt to do so came to be known, after Moore, as the naturalist fallacy. One of the implications of Putnam's rejection of the fact-value dichotomy is that the entire problem about the naturalist fallacy becomes insignificant.

[2] As Putnam writes, "... pragmatism has been characterized by *antiscepticism*: Pragmatists hold that *doubt* requires justification as much as belief (Peirce drew the famous distinction between 'real' and 'philosophical' doubt); and by *fallibilism*: Pragmatists hold that there are no metaphysical guarantees to be had that even our most firmly held beliefs will never need revision. That one can be both fallibilistic *and* antisceptical is perhaps *the* basic insight of American Pragmatism" (1995, 20-21).

[3] Interestingly Kant himself did not try to extend his epistemological insights to the realm of morality. Thus his first critique (*Critique of Pure Reason*) and second critique (*Critique of Practical Reason)* seem to rely on somewhat independent grounds. Putnam's unique contribution in the moral realm is bringing the insight of Kantian epistemology to the realm of morality.

8
Bibliography

This bibliography contains only works referred to in the text. A full bibliography of all of Putnam's writing until 1995 can be found at the end of Putnam 1995.

Anderson, D. L. 1992 "What is Realistic About Putnam's Internal Realism?" *Philosophical Topics* 20:1, 49-83.

Boer, S. 1985 "Substance and Kind: Reflections on the New Theory of Reference" *Analytical Philosophy in Comparative Perspective*, eds. B. K. Matilal and J. L. Shah, Dordrecht: Reidel Publishing Co., 103-150.

Clark, P. and B. Hale (eds) 1994 *Reading Putnam* Oxford: Blackwell.

Frege, G. 1967 "The Thought: A Logical Inquiry" *Philosophical Logic*, ed. P. F. Strawson, Oxford: Cambridge University Press, 17-38.

----------- 1970 "On sense and Reference" *Translations From the Philosophical Writings of Gottlob Frege*, eds. P. Geach and M. Black, Oxford: Basil Blackwell, 56-78.

Kripke, S. 1980 *Naming and Necessity* Cambridge, MA: Harvard University Press.

Passmore, J. 1988 *Recent Philosophers* London: Duckworth.

Putnam, H.1957 "Three-valued Logic" in Putnam 1975a, 166-173.

-------------1960 "Minds and Machines" in Putnam 1975b, 362-384.

-------------1962 "It ain't necessarily so" in Putnam 1975a, 237-249.

-------------1965 "Philosophy of Physics" in Putnam 1975a, 79-92.

-------------1975a *Mathematics, Matter and Method: Philosophical Papers.* Vol. 1 Cambridge: Cambridge University Press.

------------ 1975b *Mind Language and Reality: Philosophical Papers.* Vol.2 Cambridge: Cambridge University Press.

-----------1978 *Meaning and the Moral Sciences* London: Routledge and Kegan Paul.

-----------1981 *Reason, Truth and History.* Cambridge, London: Cambridge University Press.

----------- 1983 *Realism and Reason: Philosophical Papers.* Vol.3 Cambridge, London: Cambridge University Press.

------------ 1987 *The Many Faces of Realism* La Salle, Illinois: Open Court.

-------------1988 *Representation and Reality* Cambridge, MA: Bradford

Books.

------------- 1988a "Bringing Philosophy Back to Life" in *US News and World Report*, April 25.

------------- 1989 "Model Theory and the 'Factuality' of Semantics" *Reflections on Chomsky*, ed. A. George, Oxford: Basil Blackwell, 213-232.

--------------1990 *Realism With a Human Face* ed. J. Conant. Cambridge: Harvard University Press.

--------------1992 *Renewing Philosophy* Cambridge, MA: Harvard University Press.

--------------1994 Entry "Putnam, Hilary" into *The Companion to the Philosophy of Mind* ed. S. Guttenplan Cambridge, MA: Blackwell, 507-513.

--------------1994a "The Dewey Lectures 1994" *The Journal of Philosophy* XCI: 9, 445-517.

--------------1994b "Comments and Replies" in Clark and Hale (eds), 242-295.

--------------1994c *Words and Life* ed. J. Conant Cambridge, MA: Harvard University Press.

--------------1995 *Pragmatism: An Open Question* Oxford: Blackwell.

--------------1999 *The threefold Cord: Mind, Body, and World* New York: Columbia University Press.

Quine, W. V. O. 1951 "Two Dogmas of Empiricism." *From a Logical Point of View*, New York: Harper and Row, 20-46.

Redhead, M. 1994 "Logic, Quanta, and the Two-slit Experiment" in Clark and Hale (eds), 161-175.

Rorty, R. 1980 *The Philosophy and the Mirror of Nature* Oxford: Basil Blackwell.

-------------1982 *Consequences of Pragmatism* Minneapolis: University of Minnesota Press.

-------------1993 "Putnam and the Relativist Menace" *The Journal of Philosophy* XC: 9, 443-461.

Ryle, G. 1949 *The Concept of Mind* London: Hutchinson.

Smart, J. J. C. 1962 "Sensations and brain Processes" *The Philosophy of Mind*, ed. V. C. Chappell, Englewood Cliffs, N. J.: Prentice Hall, 160-172.

Salmon, N. U. 1982 *Reference and Essence* Oxford: Basil Blackwell.

Wright, C. 1988 "Realism, Antirealism, Irrealism, Quasi-Realism" *Midwest Studies in Philosophy*, Vol. 12: *Realism and Antirealism*, eds. P. A. French, T. E. Uehling and H. K. Wettstein, Minneapolis: University of Minnesota Press, 25-49.